SETH EASTMAN'S MISSISSIPPI

SETH EASTMAN'S MISSISSIPPI
A LOST PORTFOLIO RECOVERED

John Francis McDermott

UNIVERSITY OF ILLINOIS PRESS · URBANA · CHICAGO · LONDON

To Mary Stephanie

Preface

NEARLY TWO DECADES AGO, while I was gathering material for *Seth Eastman, Pictorial Historian of the Indian,* I found in the Charles Lanman Papers at the Library of Congress a letter from Eastman at Fort Snelling, dated 1 November 1847, in which the captain mentioned to his fellow painter that he had completed "one hundred water coloured sketches on the Mississippi . . . from the Falls of St. Anthony to the mouth of the Ohio." To my sorrow I could find no trace of these pictures nor any further reference to them. Later, when Bertha L. Heilbron was working on her edition of Henry Lewis's *Das Illustrirte Mississippithal,* she uncovered a letter from Lewis to his brother George in St. Louis, written from Fort Snelling on 25 September 1847, in which the panoramist declared that Eastman had one hundred and fifty such watercolors. But Miss Heilbron had no better luck than I in locating these works, nor could she find any other documentary mention of them.

It was therefore a very happy and total surprise when a descendant of one of the brothers of Henry Lewis brought into the curator's office at the St. Louis Art Museum in February 1970 an album containing eighty-one Eastman sketches, seventy-nine of them Mississippi River scenes and all but two in watercolor. (The remaining two views, one of the Hudson River from West Point, now in a private collection, and one of Cedar Keys, Florida, dated 1840, still in the possession of the Duncan family, have been omitted from this present book about Seth Eastman's Mississippi.) These pictures had been bought from Seth Eastman sometime in 1848 by Lewis, who by and by used a number of them as copy for lithographs to illustrate his book published in Düsseldorf in 1854–57. Later Lewis pasted the sketches into an album and hoped, in vain, to find a purchaser in America. At his death in 1904 his studio collection and his papers were divided among the descendants of his older brother George and their younger half-brother John. By descent the Eastman pictures came to James P. Duncan, Robert Conzelman Duncan, and Mary Lewis Duncan (Mrs. Chester D. Marquis, Jr.).

The many extant oils, watercolors, and pencil sketches by Seth Eastman and the engravings and lithographs after his work have warranted hailing him as "pictorial historian of the Indian." The reappearance of these long-lost watercolors clinch his right to the title of premier watercolorist of the Mississippi River landscape.

In preparing this book I have incurred many debts. Charles E. Buckley, director of the St. Louis Art Museum, called my attention to the Eastman pictures, encouraged my suggestion of presenting them in a book, and arranged permission for me to publish the twenty-four purchased by the museum. For the use of twenty-four more I am indebted to the generosity of the Minnesota Historical Society (of which I have been a member for at least twenty-five years) and Russell W. Fridley, its director. Thirty-one other pictures still belong to the Duncan family. I am particularly grateful to James P. Duncan (who

brought the album to St. Louis) for the right to publish these and for the very effective interest he has shown in this project.

Southern Illinois University at Edwardsville has met much of the expense of research essential to this volume. John C. Abbott, director of libraries at the university, and members of the Lovejoy Library staff have been helpful in a variety of ways. The Missouri Historical Society is always good to me beyond the call of regulations—George R. Brooks, the director, Mrs. Ernst A. Stadler, the archivist, Mrs. Fred G. Harrington, Jr., the librarian, and, in fact, the entire staff, as so often before, responded helpfully to my calls. My thanks go also to Mrs. Elizabeth Kirchner, librarian of the St. Louis Mercantile Library, for generous cooperation. The curator's staff at the St. Louis Art Museum have been more than courteous. And I have made constant use of my status of "Visiting Scholar" at Olin Library, Washington University, granted me by Andrew J. Eaton, the director, when I left the teaching staff in 1963.

Miss Bertha L. Heilbron, long my principal friend at the Minnesota Historical Society, and I have

viii

shared interest in and information about both Seth Eastman and Henry Lewis for many years. Her research and expert editorial work have been of much help in problems about these two artists. Miss Lila M. Johnson, head of the Audio-Visual Library at the society, and I have corresponded about the watercolors, and Mrs. Ruby J. Shields, chief of reference in the Manuscripts Department, and Leland R. Andrews have aided me.

Particularly important has been the cooperation of Dr. Stephen Williams, director of the Peabody Museum, Harvard University, and his assistant, Mrs. A. M. Pierce, in providing me with working prints of pencil sketches and watercolors in the Bushnell Collection which have made it possible for me to establish the source of many of the Lewis-Duncan album watercolors. I do appreciate, too, the opportunity to publish three of the Peabody's drawings among my in-text illustrations.

In this matter of identification I have once more made important use of a microfilm copy of the Minneapolis Public Library's Eastman sketchbook furnished me years ago for my earlier work on this painter. I am grateful to be allowed to publish here several sketches from it, and to Miss Betty L. Engebretsen, Minneapolis Athenaeum librarian, for her assistance in arranging this.

Miss Mildred Goosman, curator of the Western Collections at the Joslyn Art Museum, Omaha, has kindly sent me copies of Eastman drawings and watercolors for study purposes.

I am indebted also to Lindley Eberstadt, E. Coe Kerr, Jr., and John Fleming for their kind responses to my queries about some Henry Lewis material not available for use at this time.

Finally, I come to Mary Stephanie McDermott, my helpmate indeed and in fact. Many thanks once more.

John Francis McDermott

Southern Illinois University
Edwardsville
10 September 1972

ix

Contents

Illustrations

xiv

Seth Eastman and the Mississippi

NEW LAURELS must be awarded Seth Eastman: he is now to be recognized as the premier watercolorist of the Mississippi River landscape. In the mid-nineteenth century a succession of carefully studied and ably executed canvases established him as the foremost pictorial historian of the Indian. The recent coming-to-light of seventy-nine miniature watercolors of the river from the Falls of St. Anthony to a point below the mouth of the Ohio painted between 1846 and 1848, lost for a hundred and twenty-five years, confirm an early impression that he is the finest as well as the most prolific artist-recorder of the great river.

Others were before him. Samuel Seymour apparently made good use of his time on the upper river as landscape artist on Major Stephen H. Long's exploring expedition to northern Minnesota in 1823. He returned with a portfolio of drawings and watercolors, a number of which portrayed river scenes between Prairie du Chien, where the travelers "took water" northwards, and the St. Peters (now the Minnesota) River. Few of them, however, are extant and those few do not compare with the deftness and delicacy of the work of Eastman. George Catlin painted for his vast traveling gallery of the American wilderness at least twenty-five canvases depicting the Mississippi from massive, castle-like Fort Snelling to St. Louis, the metropolis of the West. He loved the spectacular and many of his scenes are dramatically effective, but few succeeded in capturing the quality of the river as do the little watercolors of Eastman.

Charles Deas, once for a little while so popular as a painter of the frontier, apparently made more than one tour from St. Louis to the north, but only one oil of Fort Snelling in 1841 remains as evidence of his activity along the river. John Caspar Wild was primarily interested not in the river but in the towns that were beginning to flourish on its banks in the early 1840s.[1]

[1] McDermott, "Samuel Seymour: Pioneer Artist of the Plains and the Rockies"; Ross, "Footnote to Indian Iconography"; Ewers, "George Catlin, Painter of Indians and the West";

For a brief moment Henry Lewis could be hailed as one of the discoverers of the romantic American landscape in the northern wilds. He returned from a painting tour in 1847 to win enthusiastic local acclaim when he showed in his St. Louis studio half a dozen "representations of some of the wildest, richest, most beautiful American scenery. . . . sketches from nature, taken in a new, wild, and by the landscape painter, unfrequented region of the country. . . . scenes out-rivaling in beauty and grandeur many of the far-famed views of Switzerland and Italy."[2] But Lewis had been seized with the idea of painting a panorama that would bring such fortune that he would not again have to worry about support for the life he had planned as landscape painter. No sooner had he finished these views of *The Falls of St. Anthony*, *Fort Snelling*, *The Gorge of the St. Croix*, and other scenes in their neighborhood than he set out on a sketching voyage on the Mississippi for his huge travelogue. After showing it in St. Louis, he departed in 1849 to exhibit it in the eastern states, Canada, and Europe, finally to settle down in Düsseldorf—to paint scenes on the Rhine.[3]

A dozen other painters of record, amateur and professional, between Seymour and Lewis, took advantage of the steamboat to make study tours up the Mississippi. John H. B. Latrobe, Charles Joseph Latrobe, Charles Lanman, Leon Pomarède, Jacob C. Ward, among them, have remained obscure, for of their sketches and paintings no more than a handful have been located and identified.

Of all these artists in the West it was Captain Seth Eastman of the First Infantry, stationed at Fort Snelling from 1841 to 1848, who was so enthralled by the Mississippi River landscape that he could capture

---

McDermott, "Charles Deas: Painter of the Frontier"; McDermott, "J. C. Wild: Western Painter and Lithographer"; McDermott, "Some Rare Western Prints by J. C. Wild."

[2] St. Louis *Missouri Republican*, 20 May 1848.

[3] McDermott, "Henry Lewis and His Views of Western Scenery" and *The Lost Panoramas of the Mississippi*, 81–144; Heilbron, ed., *Making a Motion Picture in 1848: Henry Lewis' Journal of a Canoe Voyage from the Falls of St. Anthony to St. Louis* and *The Valley of the Mississippi Illustrated*.

it so effectively for us. Top man in his art classes at the U.S. Military Academy (he was graduated in 1829), he had been trained there in topographical drawing and from 1833 to 1840 served as assistant teacher of drawing at the academy, where he himself had the opportunity of private study in landscape under Robert W. Weir. Between 1836 and 1841 he exhibited at the National Academy of Design and the Apollo Gallery in New York twenty-one oils, all but three of them Hudson River subjects. In recognition of his work the Academy of Design in 1838 awarded him a diploma as an "honorary member amateur" (amateur only because his profession was the military and honorary because he lived too many miles from New York).[4]

On 30 September 1841, after a brief period of service in Florida and sick leave in Virginia, Captain Eastman reported for duty with his regiment at Fort Snelling. This was not his first sight of the West. His initial assignment on graduation in 1829 had been to Fort Crawford at Prairie du Chien. His earliest extant view of a western scene is a pencil drawing inscribed by him: "Miss. River. Fort Crawford—Prairie du Chien 557 Miles Above St. Louis Oct. 1829."[5] After a few months he was transferred in 1830 to Fort Snelling, where he remained until November 1831. Although no other drawings of Upper Mississippi scenes for this period have been located, that Eastman was busy sketching whenever possible is evident from the finishing of two oil paintings of Fort Snelling as well as an oil *Landscape, Moonlight View of Mississippi* shown at the spring exhibition of the Academy of Design in 1838.

When he returned to Fort Snelling in September 1841, Eastman had opportunities to study at leisure the Indians of the area—chiefly Dakotas and Chippewas. He learned to speak their languages and

4 Unless otherwise acknowledged, all details about Eastman's life and work are drawn from McDermott, *Seth Eastman, Pictorial Historian of the Indian.* Only three of his Hudson River oils are located today.

5 This drawing, owned by the Peabody Museum, Harvard University, is reproduced in McDermott, *Seth Eastman*, pl. 11. Another sketch of the same view, also dated 1829, is owned by Carl S. Dentzell of Los Angeles.

to observe their customs. He persuaded them to sit for their portraits and to allow him to sketch them at their activities and their deliberations, and he took advantage of the daguerreotype to achieve accuracy in portraying their groups. Eastman kept so busy with his Indian studies that Charles Lanman, when he visited the fort in July 1846, found in his studio "about four hundred pieces, comprising every variety of scenes, from the grand Medicine Dance to the singular and affecting Indian Grave." It was an impressive sight. "When the extent and character of this Indian Gallery are considered [Lanman declared], it must be acknowledged the most valuable in the country, not even excepting that of George Catlin." The collection was so large, the visitor reported, because the artist had made no attempt to dispose of any of his Indian paintings. Except for a few that he had given to friends, "all that he ever painted are now in his possession." Eastman's thought at this time had been to hold the collection together and present it to "a distinguished college," of which he would ask only for the education of his children.[6]

[6] *A Summer in the Wilderness,* 59.

Lanman named only two of the many works in the studio, *Medicine Dance of the Dahcotah or Sioux Indians* and *Indian Burial,* and gave no hint of any landscapes in oil or watercolor. But there must surely have been many small watercolors among them. From Henry Lewis a year later we learn that Eastman then had "150 highly finish'd water colour'd drawings between here [Fort Snelling] and the mouth of the Ohio and about 80 on the Ohio." Unfortunately for the record, the steamboat which was to carry his letter to St. Louis was "ringing her bell" and the panoramist had no time to write more.[7] Exactly what was in this collection we do not know, nor do we learn anything more specific about subjects when Eastman on 1 November wrote to Lanman that he had recently proposed to sell Wiley and Putnam of New York "one hundred water coloured sketches of the Mississippi—for publication." He merely said they were "views from the Falls of St. Anthony to the mouth of the Ohio." In the meantime he had to refuse (at

[7] Henry Lewis, Fort Snelling, 25 Sept. [1847], to his brother George at St. Louis, Henry Lewis Papers, Minnesota Historical Society.

least temporarily) an offer of $1,000 for the hundred sketches from a visitor who wanted them for another publication.[8]

Nothing came of either of these proposals, but there was yet another possibility confronting Eastman. "There have been several artists here this season," he told Lanman. "It has been proposed for me to join one or two of them in Painting a panorama of the Mississippi, from the Falls of St. Anthony to New Orleans— I have not yet decided— I dislike to leave my Indian pictures— My long residence among the Indians has given me a knowledge of their habits and character. For this reason these gentlemen wish me to unite with them—" It is likely that this suggestion came from Henry Lewis. The St. Louis painter had gone north with his head buzzing with plans for his panorama. On seeing the Eastman watercolors he had written enthusiastically to his brother George that these were "the very sketches we want" and added that he had had "a first-rate offer and an important proposition" from Eastman "which may render our

affair of much more ease and importance than we thought."

Eastman did not give way to the temptation to make a fortune quickly by panorama painting. He preferred to stay with his painting of Indians and to continue in the Army. But the counter proposition which he had made, it is now clear, was to sell Lewis a quantity of his Mississippi River watercolors if the New York publisher declined them.[9]

[8] Eastman to Lanman, Fort Snelling, 1 Nov. 1847, Charles Lanman Papers, Library of Congress.

[9] In a letter to Lewis from Concord, N.H., 4 Jan. 1849, Mrs. Eastman discussed arrangements for the payment of a note Lewis had given to Eastman, obviously for the purchase of the watercolors. Eastman let Lewis have them for less than half his asking price. In a four-page manuscript list of the pictures found with the album in which Lewis many years later mounted them, the panoramist (then in Germany) wrote: "These views are all in Water Colours with one or two exceptions. There are two views which do not belong to the series—viz Ceder Keys Florida & View from West Point. The views are all about the same size 7 x 5 In with some three or four larger ones.— The whole are now bound in an Alben Would it be better to send them so, or in a portfolio.? (supposing they are sent)— My price for the whole is $400.00 What I gave the Capt[n] for them!." The letter from Mrs. Eastman to Lewis was formerly in the possession of Mrs. Emilie K. Greenough, a great-niece of Henry Lewis.

Just when the pictures passed into Lewis's hands cannot be pinpointed. It is not likely that he carried any of the watercolors away with him when he left Fort Snelling on 2 November 1847, for Eastman had not yet had an answer from Wiley and Putnam in New York. Furthermore, a number of those found in the Lewis album were painted after pencil sketches made in 1848 (the details will be noted in the catalog below). Possibly Lewis obtained the lot on the occasion of his next visit to the fort in 1848. This conjecture seems plausible when we consider a discovery made by Bertha L. Heilbron during the course of her editorial work on *Das Illustrirte Mississippithal*. On re-examining the original manuscript of Lewis's 1848 *Journal of a Canoe Voyage from the Falls of St Anthony to St Louis*, which she had published thirty years earlier, she came upon two pages of notes that had not been printed in 1936 because they had had no clear relationship to the travels recorded. But now they became significant, for they concerned an "arrangement with Mr Arst [Arnz] for a prospectus of a work on the Mississippi." Here were listed five illustrations proposed for the first number of the book:

Vignette—   Indian Funeral
First view   Perspec. of St Louis
2nd d^o Fort Armstrong Rock Is
3—   Indian deputation
4.   ~~Fort Snelling~~   Grand Turk wooding at night—[10]

When did Lewis meet Arnz? Where? The notes are not dated, but since they appear in the back of the 1848 journal, it is not unreasonable to assume that they were made sometime in that year and possibly after Lewis's return to St. Louis early in August. We may also presume that he had all five pictures at hand to show the publisher or his agent. The *View of St. Louis* was after his own 1846 composition, but the *Indian Funeral*, the *Fort Armstrong*, and the *Indian Deputation* (it will presently be made clear) were all after Eastman. *The Steamboat "Grand Turk" Wooding by Night* (plate 2 in *The Valley of the Mississippi Illustrated*) he was later to describe in that book as a representation of one of "the largest New Orleans boats wooding at night . . . below the mouth

[10] Henry Lewis Papers, Minnesota Historical Society.

of Red River. . . ." Since Lewis, to the best of our knowledge, never made a trip down the Mississippi to New Orleans and since the sketching of the lower river for the panorama was done by his assistant Rogers, this view could not have been in Lewis's hands before Rogers joined him at Galena on 21 July 1848. But the notebook entry implies that Lewis at the moment of talking with Arnz about the proposed book did have at hand both *Wooding by Night* and the three Eastmans. Yet 1848 cannot be set down as an assured date, for in this same notebook is a pencil sketch of a scene on the "Cumberland road near Weeling" which, if it is Lewis's work, must have been made much later, possibly while Lewis was on tour with the panorama in the eastern states in the spring of 1850.

There is one other possibility—perhaps the most likely. Because three of the watercolors in the Lewis collection (nos. 5, 10, and 60) were painted after drawings dated by Eastman September and October 1848, it may be concluded that the entire portfolio was brought down on the steamboat *Dr. Franklin,* which transported Company I from Fort Snelling.

Since the captain arrived in St. Louis on 7 October, about three weeks after Lewis had left for Cincinnati, it is probable that Mrs. Eastman on her way east, now acting as art agent for her husband, handed the pictures to Lewis when she stopped at Cincinnati later that month to seek the aid of the panoramist in the possible disposition of some of Eastman's oils to the Cincinnati Art Union.[11]

[11] This matter seems to be inferred from Mrs. Eastman's letter to Lewis, cited in n. 9, where the form of a note of hand which Lewis had made out to Eastman was under discussion. The St. Louis *Weekly Reveille* on 15 Sept. 1848 mentioned the expected departure of Lewis on that day. Of Captain Eastman's passage through St. Louis the *Reveille* (John S. Robb?) said in part: "Art will gain something by the change [of post], for Captain E's pencil is never idle, and as he traverses the spots made memorable by the bravery of our troops, he will not fail to place them upon his sketch book, as subjects for future hours of leisure" (8 Oct. 1848, p. 1860).

There is no mention of Arnz in St. Louis in either the *Weekly Reveille* or the *Missouri Republican* for August or September 1848, the only months when Lewis could have seen him there. The meeting could have taken place in Cincinnati during the winter of 1848–49. There is the possibility that the idea of the book was astir in Lewis's mind

What Lewis thought to do with the "water colour'd" drawings in the development of his panorama and what use he actually made of them remain unknown, for there is no further reference to the pictures in extant correspondence, no mention of them in the brief *Description of Lewis' Mammoth Panorama of the Mississippi River, from the Falls of St. Anthony to the City of St. Louis* by Charles Gayler, written to accompany the unrolling of the canvas, nor has the panorama ever been seen since its departure from Germany for India or Java in 1860.

in 1847: this would be a reasonable explanation for writing to brother George that these were "the very sketches we want." My present guess is that Lewis dealt not directly with Arnz but with an agent named Conrad Witter, a German-born bookseller of St. Louis, who was involved about this time with Hermann J. Meyer (remembered for *Meyer's Universum*, an extensive publication of engraved views of many cities and scenes about the world) and Charles A. Dana, who was to edit for Meyer in 1853–54 a two-volume work called *The United States Illustrated*—there is a tangled story in this relationship which I hope to unravel on another occasion.

Some of the watercolors may have served as studies for scenes of strong audience interest. The representations of Little Crow's village (catalog no. 22), of Wenona about to leap from her rock (no. 28), of the barracks at Fort Crawford (no. 53)—among other scenes briefly spoken of by Gayler—could have become big screen enlargements of Eastman's very small compositions (Lewis's canvas stood twelve feet high). Their availability may have lessened some of the preliminary labors for the panorama, but they would not have provided the continuity of river scene essential to Lewis's project. Furthermore, Lewis and Rogers did sketch the river from the Falls to St. Louis and the broad sweep of their extant pencil drawings show that these were the cartoons which guided the painters in the final preparation of the canvas.

But whether or not these sketches served as originals for any portions of the panorama, this is only the first part of the story of Lewis and the Eastman watercolors.

ON SETTLING in Germany in 1853 after extensive travel with the panorama, Lewis devoted much time to the book about which he had first thought in 1847 or 1848. Publication of *Das Illustrirte Mississippithal* in parts began in Düsseldorf in 1854. Collapse of Arnz and Company when only six numbers had been issued put off completion until December 1857.[12] The text was a descriptive account compiled by Lewis from a variety of largely contemporary sources mingled with observations of his own. The most impressive feature of this very substantial book was the inclusion of seventy-eight lithographs in color picturing the valley from the Falls of St. Anthony to the Gulf of Mexico. The title page announced eighty plates, but the double-page view of New Orleans was counted as two and the pictorial half title in sepia was included in the total number.

The seventy-eight numbered plates were all signed "H. Lewis, pinx."[13] The presumption would be that they were all Lewis's own original delineations. Some were. Plate 1, for example, was a greatly reduced version of Lewis's oil painting of *St. Louis, Missouri, in 1846* ("my first original," he declared in a letter to the American Art Union on submitting the canvas in 1847).[14] Plate 4 (*Fort Snelling*) was certainly his. So also were no. 19 (*The Camp of the United States Troops at Wabasha Prairie*), no. 20 (*The Indians' Grand Council*), and no. 22 (*The Indian Camp at Wabasha Prairie*). Others of the Upper Mississippi River views were possibly from his original sketches

[12] For the history of this work see Bertha L. Heilbron's admirable edition in English, *The Valley of the Mississippi Illustrated*, published in 1967 by the Minnesota Historical Society with all illustrations in color. Citations of plates and text below will be to this edition, except as otherwise noted. The society has also published the entire set of plates in 35 mm. color prints in its very handsome *General Catalogue of Publications, 1971–1972*.

[13] In the German edition. In the 1967 edition this has been reduced to "H. Lewis."

[14] McDermott, "Henry Lewis and His Views of Western Scenery." The 31⅞-by-42½-inch canvas was acquired by the St. Louis Art Museum in 1955.

and paintings. But I have already suggested in *The Lost Panoramas of the Mississippi* that Charles Rogers, his assistant on the sketching trip in 1848 from Galena to St. Louis, should be credited with the original drawings and possibly with the lost watercolors prepared for the lithographer of all the views of the river below St. Louis as well as of some above.[15] Now, with the rediscovery of the Eastman watercolors, it becomes certain that at the very least seventeen of the fifty-nine plates (including the half title) depicting scenes above St. Louis were copied by the lithographer from originals by Eastman.

Such use does not imply any impropriety on the part of Lewis in signing the illustrations in his book. The painting of panoramas was a business, a veritable industry, at which a great many theater artists and landscape painters in the mid-nineteenth century tried their hands in the generally vain hope of making real money by the brush. The man who had the idea for a panorama called in others to assist him so that he might literally get the picture on the road before a rival could crowd in with a like project.

[15] Pp. 109, 128, 192.

The assistants presumably were paid off in cash. Sometimes their names were mentioned in the program descriptions provided for the audience or in the accompanying lecture at the showing of the picture. Sometimes the assistants were named in the advertisements or in the news coverage. But they were not listed as co-authors unless they had a partnership interest in the business.

Lewis sought the assistance first of Sam Stockwell, St. Louis scenic artist, and then of Leon Pomarède, also of St. Louis (both of them later painted panoramas of their own). Apparently he tried to persuade Eastman to join in his project. In the long run Charles Rogers did much of the field sketching. For the actual laying of paint on canvas, Lewis had, in addition to Rogers, four more associates working with him in Cincinnati ("Leslie, Durang, Johnston, and Laidlaw"), providing very necessary help when we recall that the completed panorama was 1,300 yards long and 4 high. But on completion the picture became "Lewis' Mammoth Panorama" without any qualification, and in the testimonials he was called "the accomplished artist who made all the sketches of which the panorama is composed, and placed them on canvas."[16] He was not appropriating Eastman's work to pass it off as his own: he had bought the watercolors, and within the conventions of the time they had become his to use as he wished. This applies equally to *Das Illustrirte Mississippithal*. It should be remembered that he was not merely an admirer of Eastman as officer and as painter but also a very useful friend to him in promoting the sale of his pictures. Finally, we should note that the sale of the watercolors to Lewis did not stop Eastman from publication of identical sketches as illustrations for Henry Rowe Schoolcraft's *Information Respecting the Indian Tribes of the United States* as well as for several of Mrs. Eastman's volumes of Indian legends.

In addition to complimentary remarks in *Das Illustrirte Mississippithal* about both Eastmans as observers of Indian customs and character, Lewis did make specific acknowledgment of some of the captain's pictorial contributions to his book. Plate 3, representing "a deputation of Dakota Indians on their way to sign a treaty with the pale faces," Lewis announced in his third chapter, was "from a sketch by Major S. Eastman, U.S.A."[17] The lithograph was based on no. 41 in the catalog below. "In the one boat," Lewis wrote, "may be seen the flags of the United States, showing that they are treating with that government, and in the other, their own curious national standard made by fastening the tail feathers of the war eagle round a crooked stick."

Actually, however, in both the lithograph and the watercolor we see a number of canoes (six in Eastman, eight or nine in Lewis) crowding together in the river. Observing them, in the Eastman view, are two Indians (one standing, one sitting) on a sandbar beside their birch canoe in the water near them. In the Lewis plate the canoe is beached, upside down, the Indians are posed slightly differently, and in the foreground are strewn paddles, a gun, a bucket, camping rolls, three birds lately shot, and other suitable bits of Indian baggage. Mount Trempealeau and the bluffs in the background are the same; the only difference in

---

16 Heilbron, *The Valley of the Mississippi Illustrated*, 36.

17 *Ibid.*, 53.

the landscape is the prominence given two wooded islands in midstream. Thus, Lewis's plate is not a photographic duplicate of the watercolor but is a close copy of it.[18]

The second acknowledgment of an Eastman original was for the view of *Cassville, Wisconsin, in 1829* (Lewis plate 32). Of this the panoramist wrote: "The sketch was taken by Major Eastman, who was then conducting a division of troops to Prairie du Chien."[19] Eastman's original pencil drawing made in September or October 1829 is not of record. The lithograph is in every detail from Eastman's watercolor (no. 56 in the catalog below).

No other lithographs are credited to Eastman originals, but elsewhere in the book Lewis did make

---

[18] Lewis was not the only panoramist to be in Eastman's debt: John Rowson Smith also incorporated this same scene into his moving picture. It will be recalled that in his letter of 1 Nov. 1847 to Charles Lanman, Eastman wrote: "There have been several artists here this season. It has been proposed for me to join with one or two of them in Painting a panorama of the Mississippi." I think one of these artist-visitors quite possibly was Smith, whose travelogue opened at Saratoga in August 1848. Smith's picture is not extant, but, according to the program pamphlet, it contained a view of Lake Pepin showing on the right "the rocks of Maiden's Leap, 500 feet perpendicular" and in the foreground "a delegation of Indians in canoes, meeting at a sand bar, to have 'a talk' about a treaty," taken "from a splendid painting by Captain Eastman" (*Professor Risley and Mr. J. R. Smith's Original Gigantic Moving Panorama of the Mississippi River*, p. 11). The writer declared that it had been painted for the American Art Union, New York, but the extant records of the AAU do not mention it. Lewis exhibited *Indian Deputation* in his St. Louis studio in May 1848. Apparently in the fall Mrs. Eastman left it with the Cincinnati Art Union on her way east. In the 1849 distribution of the CAU, it was entitled *The Indian Treaty*. Drawn by Miss Elizabeth K. Lewis of Cincinnati, its location is unknown today. A lengthy description of it in the *Missouri Republican* for 2 May 1848 is quoted in McDermott, *Seth Eastman*, 46. Perhaps to crowd as much subject matter as possible into his panorama Smith chose to move the deputation from a spot near Mount Trempealeau to Winona's Rock in Lake Pepin. Had he, too, carried away an Eastman watercolor study for this lost canvas? For Smith, see McDermott, *Seth Eastman*, 42–43, 45–47, 230, and *The Lost Panoramas of the Mississippi*, 47–67.

[19] *The Valley of the Mississippi Illustrated*, 186. Eastman was a major at the time Lewis was writing; in 1829 he had been a second lieutenant on his first duty tour. For "division of" read "some."

14

one more bow to "Major Eastman, to whom the author of this work is indebted for numerous sketches and much information about the condition of the Indians."[20] And well he might, for his debt was large.

To begin with the beginning. For his pictorial half title Lewis chose to use Eastman's *Indian Burial* (catalog no. 16), which he copied in all details. On the watercolor one notes the trial lettering in pencil, "Der Mississippi," which arches over the group of figures just as on the printed page.

Plate 7 (*Rolling Prairie*), picturing "an Indian encampment, with a party going to the hunt [p. 77]," makes obvious use of the more prominent tepee with the pictographs on the buffalo skin and the trophies or war equipment attached to the tree stump at the extreme left of Eastman's sketch (catalog no. 18). The watercolor has no landscape background. That of the lithograph has a curious resemblance to the distance in Eastman's *View of the Prairie at Montrose* (catalog no. 64), a place far from the Sioux country. Did Lewis or his lithographer make a new picture

splicing two of Eastman's sketches? The Indian seated on the tree stump and the mounted warrior are Lewis creations; the other figures are after Eastman.

Plate 8 (*The St. Peters River Valley*) is a copy of Eastman's sketch (catalog no. 11) even to the position of the two Indians in the foreground.

Plate 10 (*St. Paul, Minnesota*), except for the addition of a number of canoes drawn up on shore and many more tiny figures indicated on the waterfront slope, and a different positioning of the Indian figures in the right foreground, is a duplicate of the Eastman pencil-and-wash sketch (catalog no. 21). The difference in drawing style and in purpose of these two artists can be observed in a pencil sketch by Lewis made on 9 July 1848 in his panorama sketchbook no. 1. His double-page spread records exactly the same view of river and town, but no one would confuse the authorship of the two pictures.[21]

Plate 11 (*Little Crow's Village*) is an exact copy of Eastman's no. 22.

Plate 12 (*Red Rock Prairie*), except for the position

20 *Ibid.*, 155.

21 Unfortunately the Lewis sketch (in a private collection) is not available for reproduction.

of the dog and the addition of one figure on the right, is a duplicate of Eastman's no. 23.

Plate 13 (*Medicine Bottle's Village*) is identical with Eastman's no. 24.

Plate 15 (*Red Wing's Village*) is identical with Eastman's no. 25.

Plate 16 (*An Indian Cemetery*) derives its principal interest from Eastman's no. 14. Though the river (the St. Peters) is more clearly pictured by the lithographer and the background is more pronounced, the burial scaffold in the plate is very like that of Eastman.

Plate 17 (*Lake Pepin*), it is interesting to discover, is not after one of the present watercolors, but that the lithograph was copied from an Eastman painting is undeniably established by a pencil sketch in the Peabody Museum identical with the Lewis illustration (figures 1 and 2).

Plate 18 (*The Maiden Rock*) is identical with Eastman's no. 27 (figures 3 and 4).

Plate 24 (*The Dog Dance*) is identical with Eastman's no. 17.

Plate 28 (*Indians Hunting Deer by Moonlight*) is a duplicate of Eastman's no. 68, but the picture has been reversed in the lithograph.

Plate 29 (*Scalping Scene on the Mississippi*) is identical with Eastman's no. 42.

Plate 30 (*Prairie du Chien, Wisconsin, in 1830*). This view of Fort Crawford is identical with Eastman's no. 53.

Plate 43 (*Fort Armstrong on Rock Island*) is identical with Eastman's no. 60.

Although they were not derived from the present collection of sketches, three other illustrations in *Das Illustrirte Mississippithal* were after the work of Eastman. The Falls of St. Anthony was one of the favorite landscape subjects of Lewis—in 1847 he painted two views on the spot and later produced other canvases from his own original sketches. Yet for plate 6 (*The Falls of St. Anthony*) he chose to use the Eastman rendering of that scene which had been

FACING PAGE: 1. *Miss. River Lake Pepin from the middle of the Lake looking South*. Pencil sketch by Seth Eastman. Peabody Museum, Harvard University.

Miss. River Lake Pepin from the middle of the Lake looking South

2. *Lake Pepin*. Lithograph.
Plate 17, Henry Lewis,
Das Illustrirte Mississippitl
(1854–57). Obviously cop
from a lost watercolor base
on figure 1. Photo courtesy
Lovejoy Library,
Southern Illinois Universit
Edwardsville.

3. *View of the Lover's Leap   1848*. Pencil sketch by Seth Eastman. The original drawing for the watercolor (no. 27 below). Minneapolis Public Library.

published as a lithograph in Mrs. Eastman's *Dahcotah* in 1849. This can be explained by the fact that the plate was of about the same size (4½ by 7¼ inches) as the *DIM* plates and therefore easy for the lithographer to copy. That Lewis had the book with him in Europe is clear from the several quotations he made from it in his text. In fact, Mrs. Eastman almost certainly gave him a copy.[22] In the German lithograph the viewing point and the position of the lone Indian are exactly those of the Eastman illustration, which derives from a pencil sketch dated July 1848 in the Peabody Museum (a watercolor from the pencil is

[22] In the letter to Lewis of 4 Jan. 1849 previously cited, Mrs. Eastman wrote that she had "requested Mʳ Wiley to allow me a few copies [of *Dahcotah*] to send to my friends—I presume he will do so, and I will certainly forward one to you as soon as the book is out." The Eastman watercolor is reproduced in McDermott, *Seth Eastman*, pl. 86.

FACING PAGE: 4. *The Maiden Rock.* Lithograph. Plate 18, Henry Lewis, *Das Illustrirte Mississippithal* (1854–57). An exact copy of Eastman's watercolor (no. 27 below). Photo courtesy Lovejoy Library, Southern Illinois University, Edwardsville.

owned by the Minneapolis Public Library). The German lithographer, however, treated the brush and bushes in the sideground more effectively than did his American counterpart.

Plate 9 (*The Little Falls*) was quite likely done after the Eastman chromolithograph *The Laughing Waters* used in *The Iris for 1852* (published in 1851) to illustrate one of Mrs. Eastman's Indian legends. Again, this would have provided a picture of a convenient size for the German lithographer to work from. Certainly plate 9 is much more like Eastman's view (minus the Indian shooting the deer) than it is like the oil study that Lewis painted on the spot in the fall of 1847, now in the Minnesota Historical Society collection and reproduced by Miss Heilbron in her edition of Henry Lewis's *Journal of a Conoe Voyage* (facing page 27).

Lewis's plate 27 (*Indians Spearing Fish by Moonlight*) is after an oil by Eastman, the location of which is unknown today. (It is likely enough that Eastman painted a watercolor of this subject, but none has ever been reported.) The canvas, then in the possession of E. R. Mason, an attorney of St.

Louis, was exhibited in that city in September 1848; in fact, a local newspaper reported, it had been painted for its owner. According to the *Missouri Republican* (16 September 1848), this "landscape gem" presented

a moonlight scene on one of the Western rivers—probably the St. Croix or the Wisconsin, and a more beautiful composition of cliffs, forest, stream, sky, and savage life, all blending in harmonious and artistic unison, and lighted up by the beams of a full moon, gushing out from behind mighty clouds, as she holds on her stately and lonely way, we have rarely looked on. Pictures of this description are said by artists to present peculiar difficulties in execution. But the water—*that* strikes one as peculiarly perfect—cool, clear, dark and deep, limpid, pellucid, almost transparent, reflecting the deep shadows of the gray old cliffs, between which and beneath which, it pours itself in its narrow race-course, and throwing back the moonbeams that stream out upon its rippling bosom. This piece combines many characteristics of the scenery of the north-western rivers. The discolored crags with the pensile parasites trailing over their broad foreheads above the rippling surface and breaking the otherwise smooth mirror in dashes of light and shade—these are all features peculiar to the upper rivers of the western

valley. And, yet, who ever has viewed the grand and gloomy scenery of the Kentucky river, will by this picture, be forcibly reminded of that. On the foreground of the picture, is a fire blazing upon a flat rock which projects into the stream. In its red glare, stands an Indian —his tall figure swathed in his blanket, engaged in spearing the fish attracted to the surface by the flame. Beside him, sits his squaw; and their birch canoe is secured by the paddle stuck into the muddy bottom.

The contrast of the flame colors with the preponderating gray of the picture is especially worthy of notice.

Henry Lewis had opportunity to see this painting—and to copy the whole scene and action—for it was exhibited in the studio he occupied with James F. Wilkins. In *The Valley of the Mississippi Illustrated* (page 167) one finds only a brief paragraph about this Indian manner of hunting with no location indicated for the scene, but that paragraph significantly is in a chapter on Chippewa customs.[23]

Having gone this far in tracing the unacknowledged

[23] The St. Louis *Weekly Reveille* also noticed the painting on 17 Sept. 1848 (p. 1835). The watercolor in the present collection (catalog no. 2) is an entirely different subject.

use of Eastman sketches in *Das Illustrirte Mississippithal*, I shall venture a not entirely preposterous query. Was Lewis indebted to Eastman for still more of his illustrations? A dozen other lithographs in that book have bluff backgrounds or portray river vistas which are strongly suggestive of Eastman's interest and treatment. Among them I point to plate 21, *The Mouth of the Chippewa River*; plate 26, *The Battle of Bad Axe*; plate 33, *The Indians' Lookout*; plate 35, *The Tete des Morts River*; plate 38, *Bellevue, Iowa*; plate 39, *Savanna, Illinois*; plate 41, *The Rapids* (at Keokuk, Iowa); plate 53, *A View on the Mississippi near Quincy*; plate 56, *Louisiana, Missouri*; plate 57, *Grafton, Illinois*; plate 61, *The Mouth of the Missouri*.

Since Eastman's original (1847) selling price for watercolors had been $10 each, the fact that Lewis later paid $400 for his lot prompts the conjecture that the panoramist may have acquired not the eighty-one pictures in the newly recovered collection but one hundred sketches—a convenient round number for the sum mentioned. With his family going to live in the East for months to come while he was on duty on the plains of Texas (he was banking on getting the appointment to illustrate the Schoolcraft volumes and on going soon to Washington), the captain was pressed for cash. He had a great quantity of watercolors for which he had no market and a superabundance of drawings from which he could (and did later) paint others. Lewis could not have afforded to buy the sketches at the $10 price and he had been active in promoting, without commission, the sale of Eastman's oils in St. Louis and Cincinnati. Why should Eastman not have been glad to let Lewis have a batch of the watercolors for a much smaller sum than he had hoped for from a publisher? Since it was only years later that the present lot of sketches were pasted into the album in which they were preserved, nineteen of them could easily have been lost or mislaid after use by the lithographer. Lewis's plates 6, 9, 17, and 29 I have already shown were based on paintings not in the Lewis-Duncan collection today. Perhaps more of the illustrations in *Das Illustrirte Mississippithal* were copies of Eastman watercolors.

Thus it is clear that at least one-fourth (and possibly

more) of the pictures in Lewis's book were after the work of Seth Eastman. But it was as well for the reputation of the army artist that his authorship remained unknown, for the crude copies of the lithographer were no compliment to the original painter. As published they were of value as historical documentation but the poor draftsmanship of the copyist lost the precision of the originals as topographic paintings and gravely compromised their artistic effectiveness. Lewis's river is an antiquarian record: Eastman's is a living landscape. Beyond this the severe limitations of color deprived the sketches of their brilliance as watercolors. It was a happy day when the originals of these views came once more to light, for they establish Eastman as an important landscape painter and an exquisite watercolorist.

III

UNTIL TODAY Eastman has been classed as a painter of Indian life and a reporter of frontier scenes. He has not been thought of as a landscapist, for, though during his years as assistant drawing master at the U.S. Military Academy he exhibited at least twenty landscapes in oil—quite enough to mark him as a promising member of the yet unnamed Hudson River school—and finished an unknown number of watercolor views near West Point, only three oils and but a handful of watercolors from that period could be located a century and a quarter later.

From the years at Fort Snelling two oil landscapes have survived. The principal lot of his works in watercolor has been a group of thirty originals in the James Jerome Hill Reference Library in St. Paul, but of these only three are true landscapes (*The Falls of St. Anthony*, *The Laughing Waters*, and *Wenona's Leap*), and even these have figures imposed to convert them into illustrations for Indian legends and customs.[24] Of the possibly two dozen finished

[24] The Hill collection numbers fifty-seven pieces from Eastman's hand, but some of these are designs of objects and

watercolors of Upper Mississippi scenes in the Peabody Museum, the Newberry Library, the Joslyn Art Museum, the Minneapolis Public Library, and other public and private collections, less than half are purely landscape. It it only in the Henry Lewis portfolio that a considerable body of work in watercolor devoted largely to landscape provides opportunity to judge Eastman's skill in this subject matter and medium.

What is immediately obvious on looking at this new-found group of pictures comes as no surprise. Eastman was a realist in his approach to landscape as he was in his studies of Indian life. An Indian man, we have long known, to him was not a noble primitive dwelling in an ideal world, he was not a dashing leader or a furious villain magnificently attired who expressed the heroic spirit of the tribe, he did not embody the elemental forces of nature; he was simply a man living in the manner and according to the customs of his people. Eastman had no editorial to deliver, no social comment to make, no romantic

others are copies by him of originals by others. The entire lot is from work for the Schoolcraft volumes.

world to reveal. He painted life beyond the frontier as he saw it lived. His Indians remained Chippewas, Sioux, Winnebagoes lounging about their daily affairs, playing their games, doing their chores, sometimes joining in ceremonials. His buffalo hunts were pictorial renditions of necessary and commonplace action, not dashing scenes of sporting adventure in a strange, fresh setting. He was painting not to thrill the stay-at-home white man with glimpses of savage ways and raw adventure in the manner of Charles Deas, not to stir him with the glamor of a summer's sporting tour in the Wild West so vividly captured by Alfred Jacob Miller, not to move him to admiration of the impressive Indian in his Sunday best as spectacle-loving George Catlin delighted in doing, but to make a careful record of the red people among whom he was stationed. Here is displayed the calm observation, the precise, sympathetic, but objective reporting of good genre art.

So it was with landscape. His concern was not with himself but with the scene before him. He sought no identification with nature, no emotional release in exploring hitherto unknown vistas in the wilderness, no excitement in a grand confrontation with the physical world about him. His purpose was to capture a view for its own sake, to realize a beautiful scene simply because it was beautiful, to record it exactly as it was. Where Washington Allston and Thomas Cole painted what they felt, Eastman painted what he saw.

A few of these seventy-nine Upper Mississippi subjects bought by Lewis with his own possible uses in mind must be put aside as not landscape at all but illustrations of Indian life. *Indian Burial* (no. 16), picturing men and women lifting a wrapped corpse onto a burial platform, is without scenic background. In the two watercolors of Indian graveyards (nos. 14 and 15) the river in the distance and the bluffs beyond it are indicated and may even be identifiable, but these are matters of no subject significance. So, too, in *Permanent Residence of the Sioux Indians* (no. 19) and in *Medicine Bottle's Village* (no. 24) interest is in the construction of the dwellings, in the Indians lying about in characteristic positions, in the performance of usual actions. The glimpses of the stream beside which the house is placed in the first and of the foliage in the second picture are appropriate but add no sense of particularity. *Dog Dance of the Sioux Indians* (no. 17) is another Indian subject for which no background is provided; attention is centered in the arrangements for the dance to be performed. *Travelling Tents of the Sioux Indians Called a Tepe* (no. 18) might be sited in any field anywhere: the artist has concentrated on showing a typical tepee with typical figures added—he has not distracted from his illustration by any sketch of scenery, which would be a matter of no point here, for he was making a representation of a usual object, not painting a specific view. Excellent as most of these pictures are in their own ways, they are not landscapes.

Several of the watercolors combine the Indian study with landscape. *Indians Killing Fish* (no. 2) is a report of a common employment, but the pleasing river view could well exist without the prominently positioned birch canoe and the Indian figures. *Little Crow's Village* (no. 22) can be looked on as a "snapshot" of an actual Indian town effectively caught by a passing traveler. Its excellent detail is so set against an impressive background of bluffs that we see at once its twofold value as document and as river scene. In contrast *Red Wing's Village* (no. 25) is a landscape featuring two mountainous hills overshadowing dwellings which have been reduced to microscopic proportions. The figures in *Indian Battle Scene* (no. 42) are no more than obvious illustration. Here Eastman has painted a fine river view (probably in the vicinity of Mount Trempealeau) which pleased him for its own sake and then imposed the figures for the purpose of showing Indians in the act of scalping fallen foes. *Indian Deputation on their Way to Washington* (no. 41)—the subject of a lost oil—again combines an Indian group with an authentic landscape, the interest equally divided between them.

In yet other pictures Indians play minor roles. Nos. 23 (*Red Rock Prairie. Indians Embarking*) and 49 (*About 20 miles above Prairie du Chien*) make use of the same group of figures, slightly rearranged. They are prominently placed across the foreground, distinctly drawn, with authentic detail of equipment, but the sketches are "landscapes with figures"—they do not become studies of Indian life. So, too, with the solitary Indians shooting wild fowl and deer in nos. 51 and 68, the Indians gathered around a campfire in no. 43, the group "on the move" with their horse-drawn travois in no. 31, the canoe being carried in no. 50, the tepee and five figures encamped at the bluff near Wabasha's Prairie in no. 36. These show Indians in characteristic pose or movement but they illustrate nothing—we see what they are doing but not how they do it. The pictures are first of all landscapes—the figures, bits of action, and representative objects merely add human life to the scene. This distinction is most obvious when we note that the tepee in no. 36 is remarkably like the nearer one in No. 18. The latter sketch, however, is solely an illustration, a record of the appearance of a typical traveling lodge, whereas no. 36 is a landscape featuring an unusual bluff with the tepee and the reclining figures an integrated minor portion of the total scene.

Very small Indian figures are found in many other of these watercolors, but their unimportance as *Indians* is evident in their tiny size. They are merely a touch of life that makes more vividly real the grand vistas and the imposing bluffs of the great river, that impress on us the quiet, solitary magnificence the painter has sought to capture. Eastman has not hesitated to re-use typical representative figures. One is a seated man, wrapped in a blanket, smoking a long pipe (nos. 21, 31, 50, 59). Another is a hunter who stands with his back to us, his gun held across his chest with the muzzle above his left shoulder (nos. 5, 8, 50, 79). No doubt basic drawings in larger size had been made in a workbook no longer existing. A seated woman, back view, with a child before her, appearing in nos. 24, 36, and 69, he had first sketched in watercolor in 1847.[25] The same small dog stands for his portrait in nos. 19, 23, 31, and 49. Such repetitions would not be acceptable in full-scale canvases of Indian life, but in these little watercolors, reduced to miniature size, the figures serve admirably to give a tone of the Indian world to the river landscape. So varied are they in arrangement, so integrated into the scenes in which they appear, so completely individual in effect, that it is only on close examination that we become aware of their re-use.

[25] Minneapolis Public Library sketchbook, page size 3¾ by 7 inches.

Two of the views can be classed as military topographical documents. *Fort Crawford, Prairie du Chien, in 1829* (no. 53), painted from a sharply drawn pencil sketch made nineteen years earlier, and *Fort Snelling in 1848* (no. 5), drawn in September 1848, are primarily representations of army installations. The landscape has not been painted for its own sake but merely to show the physical setting for the forts. The foreground slope from which we view Fort Crawford has some individual feeling, but the interest of the picture is strongly centered in the fort itself. At the right of the Fort Snelling sketch the artist has given us an enticing glimpse of the Mississippi; he has added for appropriate local color a tepee at the left, a canoe approaching shore in the center, and a steamboat tied up at the wharf toward the right, all of which suggest the varied life at such an outpost, but the picture remains a carefully drawn close-up of a mighty military structure. In contrast, *Fort Armstrong on the Mississippi—in 1848* (no. 60) is a painting for its own sake; the fort is merely the center of a pleasing view upstream. As a military document it would have had little value.

It is not possible to say with assurance how Eastman created these watercolors, for he has told us nothing of his picture-making practices. But his procedure seems obvious. He was first of all a topographic draftsman with an insatiable passion for drawing. Wherever he went he carried his sketching block. Whenever a moment permitted his pencil was at work. Even at such a tense hour as the confrontation at Wabasha's Prairie in June 1848, when his troops and their Dakota allies faced the defiant Winnebagoes, he could sit quietly sketching the encampment which the angry red men threatened to rush at the slightest excuse.[26]

Eastman must very quickly have accumulated a thick portfolio of western scenes. A few extant drawings date from 1829. A hastily made sketch of Fort Armstrong on Rock Island (September 1841) bears an identifying number 47; a view at Montrose (opposite Nauvoo) dated September 2 (or 21?) 1841 (figure 5) is numbered 48—apparently these were page numbers in a sketchbook long ago broken up.

His fecundity and his assiduity in sketching are well exemplified by the surviving portion of the pictorial report of his removal from Fort Snelling to Texas in September–November 1848. Nearly thirty drawings in the Bushnell Collection at the Peabody Museum (about half of them dated in his hand) record his farewell glimpses of the Falls of St. Anthony and of the fort where he had spent seven years in frontier duty and picture scenes long familiar to him as far down the Mississippi as Bloomington (now Muscatine), Iowa. That many other sketches made on the downriver trip to St. Louis and below have been lost or mislaid is strongly suggested by the fat sketchbook that Eastman opened at a point sixty miles below St. Louis, which is filled with sixty-seven views taken from the deck of the steamboat on the way to New Orleans, eleven more made at the mouth of the Mississippi and on the coastal voyage to Port Lavaca, and another sixty on the way into the heart of Texas in 1849.[27]

Such field work was almost entirely in pencil.

26 McDermott, *Seth Eastman*, 33–35 and pl. 29.

27 Lois W. Burkhalter, *A Seth Eastman Sketchbook.*

View from the Steamboat at Montrose (Iowa) looking
down — Sept 2? 1841

No. 320

48
X

Occasionally Eastman did use color on the spot. Of a group of twenty work sketches surviving from his teaching years at West Point, fifteen or sixteen are pencil and wash or watercolor drafts.[28] In the Minneapolis Public Library sketchbook four preliminary views of the Hudson taken in 1838 were done in color, and in the same book three or four Mississippi River scenes were also rough watercolors.

[28] These pictures were recently in the possession of M. Knoedler & Company, New York. It is interesting to note that Eastman's identifying numbers in the lower righthand corner run as high as 30 (possibly 31). One of the sketches pictures the commanding officer's quarters at Fort Jessup and therefore must have been made in 1832 while Eastman was on duty in Louisiana. Another is a rough pencil drawing of Prairie du Chien, which probably should be dated 1829–31; in detail it is very like no. 54 in the present catalog. The remaining pictures are scenes on the academy grounds or views of the Hudson close by.

FACING PAGE: 5. *View from the Steamboat at Montrose (Iowa) looking down—Sept 2 [21?] 1841.* Pencil, ink, and wash sketch by Seth Eastman. The original for No. 62. Peabody Museum, Harvard University.

Some few of the extant finished watercolors of Hudson River scenes and of views around Fort Snelling may have been completed on the spot. However, it is safe to say that Eastman's ordinary procedure was to sketch in pencil every landscape or riverscape that caught his eye and then to paint at leisure such pictures as we find in the Henry Lewis collection and other extant work. Of the "four hundred pieces" that Lanman had seen at Fort Snelling in the summer of 1846 a large number must have been watercolors. By November 1847, we are informed by Lewis, Eastman had one hundred and fifty colored views of the Mississippi and eighty more of the Ohio. In the summer of this year he had no doubt been stimulated by the prospect of sale of one hundred pictures for a "Mississippi River Illustrated" book.[29]

[29] To an army captain of twenty-four years' service whose pay and allowances came to $113.50 a month, $1,000 cash would have been sufficient temptation to busy himself with work that he could so easily turn out. It is idle to speculate about the proposed book: coffee-table productions devoted to the beauties of the American landscape had been luring artists for decades. Eastman must surely have known Joshua

However many watercolors were to be seen in Eastman's room in the fall of 1847, he continued to paint his admirable little views in 1848, for at least ten of the Henry Lewis pictures were after pencil sketches bearing that year-date (nos. 27, 28, 34, 36, 38, 39, 44, 45, 48, 49). Others in the lot acquired by the panoramist were based, again on the evidence of the Minneapolis Public Library workbook, on the drawings made in 1847. Half a dozen of the finished pictures (nos. 4, 11, 15, 65, 71, 76) were dated 1847 or 1848 by Eastman. At least three (nos. 5, 10, 60) may have been painted on the trip to St. Louis in September 1848. But some of the remaining watercolors were from sketches going back as far as 1829. On the whole, whatever the date of the original drawing, the Eastman watercolors bought by Lewis were almost certainly painted in the period 1846–1848. They were not a single lot deliberately made for the book projected in 1847. They were individual works painted in the studio at the artist's inclination from field work.

Shaw's *Picturesque Views of American Scenery* (1819–20), Jacques Gérard Milbert's *Picturesque Views of North America* (1825) and his *Itinéraire Pittoresque du Fleuve Hudson et des Parties Laterales* (1828–29), and the very popular *American Scenery* by William Henry Bartlett and Nathaniel P. Willis (1841). He must have seen John Caspar Wild's *The Valley of the Mississippi Illustrated* published in parts in St. Louis, 1841–42. And it is more than likely that he had met this industrious Swiss lithographer either in St. Louis or on the latter's visit to Fort Snelling in 1844.

IV

THE SKETCHES in this collection not merely form the most extensive and the most carefully observed visual documentation of the Upper Mississippi River that has yet been undertaken: they are individually little masterpieces of the landscapist's art. So small that they might have been painted with the aid of a jeweler's glass, so sharply distinct that the artist might have been viewing the scenes through a telescope, so sensitive in the use of atmosphere, so delicate in their tints, these pictures are a glowing triumph for their author.

Eastman would have been unhappy indeed had he succumbed to the temptation to share in the production of a giant travelogue of the river. He did not see the Mississippi as the panoramists envisioned it: one grand changing but unending scene that a traveler might drink in as he sat on the forward deck of a steamboat. For him each view was separate and complete, each a thing in itself which appealed for what it was, each painted without relation to another.

The creator of these landscapes was a topographic artist of consummate skill, able to compress essential detail into small space. His first concern—well drilled into him, no doubt, by his professional training and by professional necessity—was always with a real scene. His pictures are never to be vaguely titled *Landscape* or *Landscape with Figures* or *Landscape with Stunted Tree* because some twisted tree had moved him emotionally. They are representations of specific and particular scenes that caught the interest of the painter: *Fort Snelling from 2 Miles Below; Mount Trempe à l'eau by Moonlight from a point two miles below—Looking North; The Devil's Bake Oven and the Grand Tower.* If we today could travel the river Eastman knew in 1848, we would be able to identify without hesitation any spot he sketched or painted. His commanding bluffs were no exaggeration, no emotional restatement of nature. These were the banks of the Mississippi in his day. Those who in their mind's eye see the river meandering through a wide flood plain with gently receding hills in the far distance have only to walk along its shores near Fort Snelling today or stop anywhere at bluff top to look down at the stream below to understand instantly the actuality of Eastman's riverscapes.

As topographic presentations his pictures are filled (but not crowded) with details. Every bit introduced within these tiny limits seems exact and essential, every object was surely before his eyes as he sketched. The Falls of St. Anthony (no. 1) is not the romantic view of a waterfall so often conventionally done, but rough water rushing over a pile of real and identifiable rocks among which ordinary river debris is caught —this is no emotional interpretation, just a sharply visualized hazard. The details of construction of Fort Snelling and Fort Crawford could not be more precise. In *Little Crow's Village* (no. 22) we have not merely the Indian dwellings but also the two-story house of the U.S. agent with its fenced garden and the burial scaffolds on the hillside and the blufftop. In the most purely landscape views we have a sense that every tree and bush is represented, every stone of the bluff, every striation, every fold of rock, each densely wooded island, each fallen tree or drifting branch, even the rocks and dirt slipping down the steep hillside. Yet there is no irrelevant detail, no confusing of effect, no crowding, for each bit is exactly in its place and scaled to correct proportion in the scene recorded.

In a sense Eastman's pictures are not compositions at all: he had no wish to arrange the elements of his nature subjects, no desire to augment or diminish any aspect of the scene, no intention to interpret it emotionally for his audience. He chose attractive views that frame themselves, careful always to

determine the angle of vision that would most effectively present the scene but without any deliberate distortion of it for "art" purposes. The only evidence of free composition, that is, of matter deliberately arranged by him to make a picture, is in the introduction of minor details, such as the placing of a canoe in the water or a deer drinking at the river's edge or a tiny figure looking deep into the background. Such bits often were not in the original drawing or were repositioned in the watercolor. But they were only devices to indicate scale and to add a glimpse of life appropriate to the occasion. Always effectively handled, they were not essential to the taking of the view, which in the watercolor remained exactly as it appeared in the pencil study. No thought of "making a picture" was allowed to alter the actuality of the scene reported.

What is particularly notable about these pictures is their sureness, their authority. At every moment Eastman knew exactly what he was doing. The original drawings are so sharply penciled, so exact in the finest detail, that we are convinced of their

1847

6. *Ten Miles above Prairie du Chien looking North 1847.* Watercolor and wash drawing by Seth Eastman. The foreground in no. 51 is added interest; the river bluffs, however, are painted exactly from this sketch. Minneapolis Public Library.

7. *About 20 miles above Prairie du Chien looking North 1848.* Pencil sketch by
Seth Eastman. The foreground in no. 49 is added interest, but the river bluffs are
painted exactly from this pencil drawing. Minneapolis Public Library.

8. *The mountain that soaks in the Water, on the Miss. looking South   1848*. Pencil
sketch by Seth Eastman. The original for no. 39. Minneapolis Public Library.

Miss. River — 700 miles above St. Louis.

10½

accuracy, their faithfulness, their reality. This assurance is infused in the watercolors which reproduce the sketches afresh without variation in line or shape. The absolute truth of the original study, of his vision, reappears in the finished painting, its actuality but emphasized by the deft and sensitive handling of his brush[30] (figures 6, 7, 8, 9).

For Eastman the Mississippi was a new Hudson River flowing past spectacular bluffs and opening enticing vistas that called importunately to a painter, a new world of fresh scenery that a man living in it was impelled to paint. This is a tranquil, relaxed world, its upper reaches still Indian country with but

[30] Two of the collection (nos. 21 and 23) are pencil drawings with color applied to the figures. However, none of the finished paintings show any trace of previous use of pencil.

FACING PAGE: 9. *Miss. River 700 miles above St. Louis.* Pencil sketch by Seth Eastman. In no. 40 the men on the sandy pulling the raft ashore have been replaced by the two deer, but the bluffs on both sides of the river are identical. Peabody Museum, Harvard University.

few glimpses of man's activity, for the tribes are scattered thinly over an immense number of miles of woods and prairie. The forts at Prairie du Chien and the mouth of the St. Peters River are impressive military stations, but there is no bustle of military activity, for none is needed. The bits of violence (Indian against Indian) in nos. 30 and 42 are rare and seem almost artificial in this pictorial report. So often we see only a solitary Indian smoking his pipe comtemplatively beside a stream, a woman and child looking away into the distance, a small family group quietly on the move for its own family reasons, men silently fishing or resting on the river bank. There is little of the fresh green of spring, of the urgency of the river at high water. The relaxed yellows and browns of later summer, the pinks and mauves and purples and grays create the feeling that this region is yet one of nature, not of human beings, who after all are few.

It is, of course, a time of change, these 1840s, but change comes slowly. White men's towns are slowly advancing up the river, the Indian is slowly retreating. But clashes of any sort are few. We have seen

Eastman meeting with recalcitrant Winnebagoes at Wabasha's Prairie. A week later, from the Round Tower at the fort we watch hundreds of Sioux and Winnebago warriors ride madly over the prairie after a small band of Chippewas who have dashed in from the north and (so the rumor goes) killed a young man—but the raiders escape and we learn that the tale was only a hoax got up by an old Sioux woman.[31]

Steamboats are carrying more and more summer tourists for a visit to "Indian land" and to mighty Fort Snelling. These trips are becoming a favorite vacation cruise for the people of St. Louis and New Orleans, of Louisville and Cincinnati, of the eastern seaboard, and, increasingly, for visitors from Europe, who all want to gaze on the wild scenery of the western country thought by some to outrival that of the Rhine and Switzerland—now that they can do it comfortably in a few days' visit aboard steamboats with pleasant companionship. Aboard, too, come more and more artists looking for new worlds to paint, new scenes of strange life to sketch for their own pleasure and to interest patrons who rejoice in the expanding glories of America.

None of these painting visitors has had Eastman's opportunity—no other man of the pencil or the brush has had his long immersion in this western world, his years of living beside the river, of going back and forth upon its waters, of camping on its shores, of seeing all the many changes of sun and shadow and cloud on bluff and cove, of watching it by moonlight, of leisurely absorbing the maturing of the summer. None of the other painter-explorers has had his gift for exact portrayal of exact scene, none his great skill in drawing, his delicacy in delineation.

Seth Eastman was indeed a loving and faithful portrayer of a picturesque scenery, which he painted with brilliant clarity, elegantly perfect in the minute rendering of scenes that charmed his eye and in turn charm us. By these newly recovered bright and beautiful pictures we now recognize that he was not merely an able watercolorist in a day before watercolors were accorded much consideration but was a master of the miniature landscape and the first master of the Mississippi River scene.

[31] McDermott, "A Journalist at Old Fort Snelling," 216–217, and *The Lost Panoramas of the Mississippi*, 96–97.

Catalog

THE eighty-one Eastman sketches in the Lewis-Duncan album (seventy-nine of them Mississippi River scenes between the Falls of St. Anthony and a point twenty miles below the mouth of the Ohio, one of the Hudson River near West Point, and one of Cedar Keys, Florida) were originally separate drawings. At some time subsequent to his use of a portion of the pictures as copy for lithographs for *Das Illustrirte Mississippithal*, Lewis pasted the entire lot into an album 13½ by 10¼ inches with a cover label reading:

> Sketches on the Mississippi from the
> Falls of St Anthony to St Louis
> by Lt Col S Eastman   U.S. Army
> made in the years 1847 | 48 | 49

On the inside of the back cover was written: "80 Studies on the Upper Mississippi made by Lt Col S. Eastman U S A in the years 1847 | 48 | 49."

Lewis numbered in pencil most, but not all, of the sketches—the highest numbers assigned being 71 and 72 for the Hudson River and Florida views. A few had no number at all; sometimes a number was used twice (e.g., 24 and 24ᵃ). With the album when it was recently rediscovered was a four-page record (in Henry Lewis's hand) headed: "List of drawings made by Lt Col S. Eastman U S A on the Mississippi in the years 1846/7/8." Here the views were numbered from 1 to 78 but four numbers were used twice and three others not at all. The numbers on the "List" frequently did not correspond with those in the album, though obviously made for the same group of pictures.

Lewis also added descriptive captions which can generally be identified as his on the basis of handwriting and orthography. Spelling was not his forte. *Prairie*, for example, was frequently written *prarie*. In the place name *Prairie du Chien*, the last word was variously spelled *Chein, Chain, Chane, Chaen, Shoen*, as well as *Chien*. Furthermore, though the writing will not show in reproductions and is indeed faint to read on the white space below the mounted pictures, he sometimes rewrote his notations. His phrases at first glance seem to fix precisely the location of some views which do not have scenic features sufficiently marked for their identification today. For a number of these watercolors, however, original pencil sketches exist which bear in Eastman's hand captions which do not agree with Lewis's. For example, sketch no. 45 in this catalog was labeled by Lewis "25 Miles above Prairie du Chain"; an identical pencil drawing, dated 1848, in the Minneapolis Public Library's Eastman sketchbook bears the legend by Eastman: "60 miles above Prairie du Chien looking North." Since Eastman's military training would stress precision in his representation of places, I prefer to accept his notations over those of Henry Lewis, whose interest as landscapist was in the scene more than the geographical location. Furthermore, Eastman wrote his legends immediately, whereas Lewis apparently added his many years later when he wanted to sell the pictures and when he had been long away from the Mississippi Valley.

On consideration of these confusions and variations about the arrangement of the Henry Lewis album pictures and of the fact that the album has been dismantled and its contents distributed among several owners, I have abandoned all numbers previously used and have arranged the pictures in a geographical sequence from the Falls of St. Anthony (with a side excursion up the St. Peters [Minnesota] River) to the last view below the Ohio, using the best evidence available for determining the order of the pictures. Whenever Eastman supplied a legend either on the here-published sketches or on a pencil original, I have chosen that as title. Otherwise I have used the geographical designation or, as a last resort for many of them, Lewis's caption.

In this catalog I have assigned a plate number, given a title, stated the medium used, noted the size of the picture in inches (height by breadth), and cited ownership at the time of compiling my list (January 1972). Since thirty-one of the paintings are still jointly owned by three members of the Duncan family (Robert Conzelman Duncan, James P. Duncan, and Mary Lewis Duncan [Mrs. Chester D. Marquis, Jr.]), in whose possession the album rested for many years, I have simplified reference to their ownership of the individual pictures by designating them as Duncan Family.

I have added details pertinent to the history or use of the individual sketches.

1. *The Falls of St. Anthony.* Watercolor, 4¾ x 7¹⁄₁₆. St. Louis Art Museum.

Below the picture is written in Lewis's hand: "No. 1. Falls of Sᵗ Anthony. (This is your possession!)." Evidently he intended the sketch as a gift to the person (probably one of his brothers in the United States) to whom he planned to send the collection for sale. Since the album including this picture was in his studio in Düsseldorf at the time of his death in 1904, it is clear that he never actually shipped the lot to America.

This view is essentially the same as that Eastman used later for plate 28 in the second volume of Schoolcraft's *Indian Tribes* and for a chromolithograph in Mrs. Eastman's *Chicora*, except that in both of these he added the rocks in the foreground and the Indian figures illustrating a legend of the Falls. The Peabody Museum has a very rough pencil drawing of the main portion of the rocks in no. 1. The watercolor in the James Jerome Hill Reference Library collection is a different composition. For the latter there is an excellent pencil sketch, dated July 1848, in the Peabody Museum.

2. *Indians Killing Fish. View on the Miss[issippi] River 4 miles above Fort Snelling.* Watercolor, 4½ x 7¼. Minnesota Historical Society.

Lewis entitled this "Indians Spearing Fish 3 Miles below Fort Snelling." However, the watercolor is essentially the same as a pencil sketch in the Peabody Museum from which I took this caption (reproduced in McDermott, *Seth Eastman*, plate 40).

3. *View below the Falls of St. Anthony Looking down the Mississippi.* Watercolor, 4½ x 7½. Minnesota Historical Society.

Lewis wrote below this picture: "The view is taken from near Sᵗ Anthony." On the accompanying list: "View near the Falls of Sᵗ Anthony." Fort Snelling was seven miles below the Falls.

4. *Fort Snelling from 1 Mile Above.* Watercolor, 4¼ x 7. Minnesota Historical Society.

Lewis's caption read: "Distant view of Fort Snelling, 1848." But immediately below on the drawing to the left is the signature "Col S. Eastman U.S.A." and on the right the date "1847." The "Col" extends beyond the left edge of the watercolor; it was obviously added by Lewis at a later time. The correctness of the date is established by a pencil drawing in the Minneapolis Public Library sketchbook, where the notation in Eastman's hand reads: "Fort Snelling from 1 mile above the Fort 1847." Pencil drawing and watercolor are identical except for the foreground Indian interest, which Eastman added in the latter. A very similar watercolor view is in the Northern Natural Gas Company Collection in the Joslyn Art Museum, Omaha.

5. *Fort Snelling in 1848*. Watercolor, 8½ x 11¼. Minnesota Historical Society.

With minor changes by the lithographer (but none for the better), this view was used as a frontispiece to Mrs. Eastman's *Dahcotah*. The original pencil sketch for this is one in the Peabody Museum bearing the legend "Miss. River. Fort Snelling 867 miles above St. Louis Sept. 1848." The tepee on the left and the canoe being dragged ashore on the right are added details in the watercolor.

It is interesting to note that Lewis apparently carried the Eastman watercolors with him on his travels. In 1851, then touring with his panorama in Canada, he supplied Paul Kane with a pencil copy of this view of Fort Snelling, which the latter used for background to his *Sioux Scalp Dance*. Addressing

"Friend Kane" from Montreal on 4 July, he wrote: "When I left your studio some months back to go and get my sketch book I found the boat just ready to start . . . consequently . . . I did not come back again to show you the drawing of the fort. I now send you by the hand of our old friend Hermitenger [?] (surnamed the 'Bishop') a slight sketch of Fort Snelling which may help you a little. . . ." The drawing was made on a page of his letter. This pencil sketch was published by David I. Bushnell, Jr., in *Sketches by Paul Kane in the Indian Country, 1845–1848*; the letter is in the Bushnell Seth Eastman Collection in the Peabody Museum.

6. *View from Tower at Fort Snelling looking North West*. Watercolor, 4¼ x 7.

This picture seems almost identical with a pencil sketch in the Peabody Museum bearing the legend I have used here. The foreground details on the left and the buffaloes on the right have been added. Lewis had called this "View below St Anthony near Fort Snelling."

7. *View from Tower [at] Fort Snelling looking* up *the [Mississippi] River*. Watercolor, 4¾ x 7. Minnesota

Historical Society.

Lewis's caption. But this is the same view as no. 6, with the painter standing closer to the clump of trees at the water's edge in the first picture.

8. *View from Tower at Fort Snelling Looking West.* Watercolor, 4 x 6½. Minnesota Historical Society.

Title from a pencil sketch in the Peabody Museum. Lewis's caption: "The Prairie back of Fort Snelling."

9. *Pilot Knob from Fort Snelling.* Watercolor, 4¼ x 7. Minnesota Historical Society.

Lewis's caption: "Pilots Knob   Mouth of the St Peters River." Mine is from a pencil sketch in the Peabody Museum, identical with the watercolor. This landmark hill was southeast of Fort Snelling, across the St. Peters, and beyond Mendota.

10. *The St. Peters River near its Confluence with the Mississippi.* Watercolor, 4½ x 7¹⁄₁₆. Duncan Family.

Lewis's caption. Identical with a pencil drawing bearing the legend "Mouth of the St. Peters. 867 Miles above St. Louis   Sept 1848" (Peabody Museum —reproduced in McDermott, *Seth Eastman*, plate 56). The Indian seated at the water's edge was added in the watercolor.

11. *The Valley of the St. Peters from Fort Snelling.* Watercolor, 4¼ x 7. Minnesota Historical Society.

Title is from a pencil sketch in the Peabody Museum. The watercolor is dated, below the picture and to the right, 1848. The Indian figures are added. Lewis's plate 8 is an identical copy. Eastman used this view for plate 24 in volume II of Schoolcraft's *Indian Tribes;* the latter engraving was also published in Mrs. Eastman's *Chicora.*

12. *Prairie near the Mouth of the St. Peters. Buffalo Hunt.* Watercolor, 4¼ x 7. Minnesota Historical Society.

Lewis's caption.

13. *View on the St. Peters 7 Miles from the Mouth.* Watercolor, 4⁷⁄₁₆ x 7⅛. Duncan Family.

Lewis's caption. A pencil sketch of this scene in the Peabody Museum bears the legend "Distant view of Fort Snelling. 7 miles above on the St. Peters," but the fort is so distant as not to be visible on an available small photograph. The sharp-pointed hill on the horizon toward the right is probably Pilot Knob; the fort would be in the center distance something to the left of Pilot Knob as we face the scene.

14. *Indian Burial Place near Fort Snelling.* Watercolor, 4½ x 7½. Duncan Family.

Lewis's caption. The scene is on the St. Peters. On the horizon between the two scaffolds Pilot Knob can be picked out. A watercolor, owned in 1961 by Kennedy Galleries, New York, and reproduced in McDermott, *Seth Eastman*, plate 32, is, with minor exceptions, a duplicate of no. 14. A pencil sketch in the Peabody Museum featuring a single burial platform much like the nearer one in these watercolors bears the legend "View of an Indian Graveyard 7 miles above Fort Snelling on the St. Peters, looking down the River towards Fort Snelling" (McDermott, *Seth Eastman*, plate 31). Although the treatment of landscape background in Lewis's plate 16 is quite different, the scaffold there looks as if it were redrawn from Eastman.

15. *Indian Graves at the Mouth of the St. Peters.* Watercolor, 4¼ x 7. Minnesota Historical Society.

The caption is Lewis's. Immediately below the picture on the left is the signature "S. Eastman 1847." The background is too sketchy for sure identification. However, a rough pencil drawing in the Peabody Museum, inscribed by Eastman "Indian Graves on Pilot Knob Opposite Fort Snelling," supplies the probable location. Perhaps these are the scaffolds we can make out on the top of the hill in no. 9.

16. *Indian Burial.* Wash drawing, 8¾ x 6½. Duncan Family.

Lewis called this "Indian Burial Ground." On the verso: "For title page." He used this sketch for the half title in *Das Illustrirte Mississippithal.* Arched over the picture one can see tentative lettering: "Der Mississippi." Eastman had just completed his oil of this subject (from which I have taken my title) at the time of Lewis's visit to Fort Snelling in 1847; a pencil study for it is in the Peabody Museum (see McDermott, *Seth Eastman*, plates 35 and 36). Three figures on the left in the oil were omitted from this watercolor and from Lewis's sepia half title.

17. *Dog Dance of the Sioux Indians.* Watercolor, 4½ x 7. Minnesota Historical Society.

On the verso: "Medicine dance of the Sioux or Dahcotah Indians on the St Peters River—near Fort Snelling. August 9th, 1847." Lewis's plate 24 is an identical copy. On the dog dance Lewis quoted both Mrs. Eastman and the captain (*The Valley of the*

Mississippi Illustrated, 154–155). This composition is quite different from the dog dance pencil sketch in the Peabody Museum and the James Jerome Hill Reference Library watercolor (McDermott, *Seth Eastman*, plates 42 and 78) from which the engraving for Schoolcraft, *Indian Tribes*, volume II, plate 22, was made. The unlocated oil listed in the 1848 distribution of the American Art Union was almost certainly this second composition (McDermott, pp. 53–54, 101, 231). My plate 106 reproduces the 1868 variant of the latter painted for the Capitol in Washington.

18. *Travelling Tents of the Sioux Indians Called a Tepe.* Watercolor, 4⅜ x 7¹⁄₁₆. St. Louis Art Museum.

In plate 7, *Rolling Prairie*, Lewis has certainly used the tepees of Eastman's watercolor and the weapons or trophies attached to the tree stump on the left; the seated figures are also Eastman's. The prairie background supplied in the lithograph has an odd resemblance to that in no. 64 below, *View of the Prairie at Montrose near Nauvoo*. The seated man and the warrior on horseback in plate 7 as well as the two buffaloes scampering away on the right are Lewis's contribution.

19. *Permanent Residence of the Sioux Indians.* Watercolor, 4¼ x 7. Minnesota Historical Society.

Probably one of the Sioux villages on the St. Peters River.

20. *Fort Snelling from 2 Miles Below.* Watercolor, 4¼ x 7. Minnesota Historical Society.

The south face of the fort from a point rather high up the slope of Pilot Knob. The Peabody Museum has a watercolor almost identical in detail but it is not a finished painting. In the Northern Natural Gas Company Collection (Joslyn Art Museum) is a pencil variant of this scene taken much closer up. To his caption (above) Lewis added: "the Bluff on the right is the Site [of the] City of Sᵗ Pauls." That spot, however, was actually six miles below the fort. See no. 21 below.

21. *St. Paul, Minnesota.* Pencil and wash, 5⅜ x 7⅝. Duncan Family.

Lewis's caption was "View of the Site of St. Paul, Minnesota, as it appeared in 1849," but this date is impossible, for Lewis last saw that town on 9 July 1848, the day he made a pencil drawing of it from his boat, the *Menehaha*. Eastman's last sight of St. Paul

49

was early in October 1848. Lewis's plate 10 shows a number of canoes drawn up on shore and, scattered before the lower buildings, more than thirty small figures which are not in Eastman's sketch. The position of the seated figure in the right foreground of the lithograph has been slightly altered but otherwise Lewis's illustration is an exact copy of Eastman's picture. In 1900 Lewis used this sketch for an oil now in the collection of the Minnesota Historical Society.

22. *Little Crow's Village on the Mississippi.* Watercolor, 4½ x 7. Minnesota Historical Society.

Miscaptioned by Lewis "Little Crow's Village on the Sᵗ Peters" but correctly identified on the verso. Also known as Kaposia. The scene is four or five miles below St. Paul on the west bank of the Mississippi, near the outskirts of present-day South St. Paul (Heilbron, *The Valley of the Mississippi Illustrated,* 92). Lewis's plate 11 (*Little Crows Village*) is an exact copy. The Peabody Museum has a rough pencil sketch inscribed "Little Crow's village looking down" and a quite finished one very like no. 22, which bears the legend "Miss. River— Indian Village (Little Crow's) 853 miles above St. Louis."

23. *Red Rock Prairie. Indians Embarking.* Pencil and wash, with color in costumes only, 5⅜ x 7 ¾. Duncan Family.

Immediately below the picture at the extreme right is a signature: "H. Lewis 1848." Was this an actual drawing by Lewis or was the inscription intended for a signature to the lithograph? The precision of the drawing and the depiction of the Indians suggest that this, too, is an Eastman sketch and not a Lewis drawing by chance included with the album lot. Lewis's plate 12 (*Red Rock Prairie*) is, with such very minor changes as the position of the dog and the adding of a figure pulling the empty canoe ashore, an exact copy. Miss Heilbron locates this spot on the eastern shore of the Mississippi about two miles below Little Crow's village and near present-day Newport, Minnesota (*The Valley of the Mississippi Illustrated,* 100).

It is interesting to note the almost identical likeness of the Indian group with that in no. 49 below (*About 20 miles above Prairie du Chien Looking North*). Except for the man on the extreme left and the omission of the gun and some other bits of equipment, all figures and groupings in this watercolor are the same as those in Lewis's plate 12. If Lewis actually made this sketch, as possibly implied by the signature, then he obviously lifted the Indian figures from no. 49. For further use of this material see the notes on the latter watercolor. In 1902 Lewis sent to St. Paul a painting entitled *Red Rock Prairie*, presumably based on this sketch; this oil has disappeared from the record.

24. *Medicine Bottle's Village*. Watercolor, 4½ x 7. Minnesota Historical Society.

Captioned by Lewis "Good Roads Village–Sious." On the verso: "Indian village on the Mississippi near Fort Snelling." This is the original for Lewis's plate 13 (*Medicine Bottle's Village*), identical in all details. This Dakota village was seven miles below Red Rock Prairie at present-day Pine Bend, Minnesota, on the west side of the Mississippi (Heilbron, *The Valley of the Mississippi Illustrated*, 105). The scene is similar to but not the same as that represented in the *Dakota Village* watercolor in the James Jerome Hill Reference Library collection, painted for the engraving in Schoolcraft, *Indian Tribes*, volume 11, plate 29.

25. *Red Wing's Village*. Watercolor, 4¾ x 8½. Minnesota Historical Society.

For reasons known only to him, Lewis captioned this sketch "Good Roads Village   Red Stone Prairie." On the verso a note describes the scene as "Red Wings village 70 miles below the Falls of St Anthony." The Peabody Museum has a finished pencil sketch inscribed in Eastman's hand: "Miss. River. Indian Village (Red Wing's) 812 miles above St. Louis" (see McDermott, *Seth Eastman*, plate 57). It shows canoes drawn up on shore which are omitted in the watercolor. Lewis's plate 15 is an exact copy of the latter. A preliminary pencil drawing in the Peabody Museum, spread over two pages, bears the legend "Red Wing's village (Sioux) 65 miles below Fort Snelling and 25 miles below St. Croix River   looking down river   View continued on opposite side [page]." The village was about four miles above Lake Pepin on the west bank of the Mississippi at the mouth of Cannon River (the present-day city of Red Wing, Minnesota). The hill on the left was called La Grange or Barn Bluff (Heilbron, *The Valley of the Mississippi Illustrated*, 111, 114–115). An oil, *Barn Bluff at Red Wing*, sent by Lewis to St. Paul in 1902, now lost, was almost certainly painted after no. 25.

26. *Hill near Red Wing's Village on the Miss[issippi] looking North.* Watercolor, 4¼ x 7. Minnesota Historical Society.

Lewis's caption was "View on the Mississippi 70 miles below the Falls of St Anthony." Mine is taken from a faint pencil sketch in the Minneapolis Public Library sketchbook where the drawing is dated 1847. Possibly another view of Barn Bluff?

27. *View of the Lover's Leap.* Watercolor, 4⅜ x 7. Duncan Family.

This sketch was oddly miscaptioned by Lewis: "Twenty miles below Wabashaw's Prairie," for his plate 18 (*The Maiden's Rock*) is identical with this watercolor. On the verso it is titled "Wenona's Rock on the Mississippi." My title is from an 1848 pencil drawing in the Minneapolis Public Library sketchbook. This bluff is on the east side of Lake Pepin about halfway down and about sixty miles *above* Wabasha's village.

28. *Lover's Leap on the Miss[issippi] looking North.* Watercolor, 4¼ x 7. Minnesota Historical Society.

Lewis's caption was "Maiden's Leap. Lake Pepin." Mine is from a pencil drawing in the Minneapolis

Public Library sketchbook, dated 1848. Another, more finished, pencil sketch in the Peabody Museum bears the legend "775 miles above St. Louis Miss. River. Lovers Leap—or Winona's Rock— on Lake Pepin. 1848." There are only minor variations in these several sketches. Eastman used no. 28 for a lithograph in Mrs. Eastman's *Dahcotah* (facing p. 165). A more dramatic version, with many Indians looking across the river at Winona about to leap off the bluff, is the watercolor in the James Jerome Hill Reference Library collection (McDermott, *Seth Eastman*, plate 95), from which was made the chromolithograph in *The Iris for 1852*, again illustrating Mrs. Eastman.

29. *Miss[issippi] River Lake Pepin from the middle of the Lake looking South.* Watercolor, 4½ x 7½. Duncan Family.

Lewis oddly captioned this "Lake Pepin looking down or North" but in the Peabody Museum there is a pencil sketch of this view with the legend I have used. Lewis's lithographer in his plate 17 must have been copying an Eastman watercolor now lost. See figures 1 and 2 in the text above.

30. *View on the Miss[issippi]—160 Miles above Prairie*

du Chien. Watercolor, 4⅜ x 7. St. Louis Art Museum. Lewis's caption in the album. His mileages are uncertain. I suggest this view is between Lake Pepin and Wabasha's village.

31. *On the Miss[issippi] 140 miles above Prairie du Chain. Indians on the Move.* Watercolor, 4⅜ x 7. Duncan Family.

Again, Lewis's caption in the album. In the "List" one sketch was called "Indians Moving Camp." The view is probably somewhere between Lake Pepin and Wabasha's village.

32. *View 125 miles above Prairie du Chien.* Watercolor, 4½ x 7⅛. Duncan Family.

Lewis's caption. Another sketch in the area above Wabasha's village?

33. *View 120 miles above Prairie du Chien.* Watercolor, 4⁷⁄₁₆ x 7⅛. Duncan Family.

In the album Lewis wrote: "View five miles below No. 32," which is no. 32 in this catalog. I think this is probably the same view as that in a badly rubbed pencil sketch in the Peabody Museum with the legend "120 Miles above Prairie du Chien Wisconsin."

34. *Six Miles above Wabasha's Prairie, Looking North.* Watercolor, 4⁷⁄₁₆ x 7⅛. Duncan Family.

In a Minneapolis Public Library sketchbook pencil drawing with this legend, dated 1848, the bluffs look much like those in this watercolor. Lewis had captioned the sketch "View a few miles below Wabashaw's Prarie."

35. *Wabasha's Village at Wabasha's Prairie. 140 miles above Prairie du Chien looking S. W.* Watercolor, 4½ x 7. Minnesota Historical Society.

This view Lewis rather oddly captioned "Wabashaw's Village—Winnebago's Indians," possibly because he recalled being there with Captain Eastman when he settled a difficulty that had arisen in June 1848 during removal of the Winnebagoes to a reservation north of Fort Snelling (McDermott, *Seth Eastman*, 33–35). On the verso is the notation "Wah-ba-sha (chief of the Sioux) village on the Miss. River 650 miles above St Louis." My title is from an 1847 pencil sketch in the Minneapolis Public Library sketchbook. In the Northern Natural Gas Company Collection at the Joslyn Art Museum, Omaha, there is another watercolor, same size, nearly identical with no. 35. This village was on the

Minnesota side of the Mississippi at the site of the present city of Winona, about forty miles below Lake Pepin.

36. *Bluff at Wabasha's Prairie.* Watercolor, 4½ x 7. Minnesota Historical Society.

Lewis had captioned this sketch "Curious Bluffs. Wabashaws Prarie." My title is from the pencil study in the Minneapolis Public Library sketchbook, there dated 1848. Except for a few differences the pencil original and the watercolor are identical. This pyramidal bluff is the principal feature in the background of the warlike sketch he made of the incident of June 1848 (Peabody Museum—reproduced in McDermott, *Seth Eastman,* plate 29), but there the river bottom is shown to be much broader. Lewis's illustrations (plates 19 and 22), which also feature this bluff, were, I think, his own work. On his way downriver in 1848 Eastman made yet another sketch of this "curious bluff" which bears the legend "Miss. River. Wahbasha's Prairie— 725 miles above St. Louis. looking West. Oct. 1848." It, too, is in the Peabody Museum.

37. *Beson's Bluff Opposite Wabasha's Prairie.* Watercolor, 4⅜ x 7⅛. St. Louis Art Museum.

Lewis's caption. The view is on the east bank of the Mississippi.

38. *Five Miles above Mount Tremble l'eau—looking South 1848.* Watercolor, 4⅜ x 7. St. Louis Art Museum.

In the album Lewis captioned this "Castle Rocks 110 miles above Prarie du Chein." My title is taken from a faint pencil drawing in the Minneapolis Public Library sketchbook. There the bluffs, particularly the rocks capping that to the right, look much like those of the watercolor, a fancied semblance to those of a castle ruin on a hilltop. In the pencil drawing a deer is on the shoreline, drinking. The shore in the foreground and the Indian figures are added in the watercolor.

39. *The Mountain that Soaks in the Water on the Miss[issippi] looking South.* Watercolor, 4⅜ x 7. Duncan Family.

Captioned by Lewis "Mount Trempe à leau." My title is from an 1848 pencil drawing in the Minneapolis Public Library sketchbook, which shows only the standing figure in the canoe but is otherwise identical. Mount Trempealeau, as the name now appears on maps, is about eleven miles below the city of Winona, Minnesota (the site of Wabasha's village) but on the east side of the Mississippi. One finds the name of this landmark variously spelled, for example, *Trombolo*, and even *Strombolo*. See also nos. 40, 41, 42, and 43.

40. *Landscape with Deer in Foreground.* Watercolor, 4⅜ x 7¹/₁₆. St. Louis Art Museum.

Lewis's caption was "Six Miles below Wabashaws Prairie." I have borrowed for this picture the title of an oil 25 by 35 painted in 1848, offered to and declined by the American Art Union in 1849. It was described by Mrs. Eastman in a letter to Warner of the AAU, 27 June 1849, as "another view" of the "mountain that soaks in the water [Mount Trempealeau]"—a picture of the same view and size, she wrote, as one that the captain had sold in St. Louis in the summer of 1848 for $100 (McDermott, *Seth Eastman*, 55, 232). If I am right in looking on this watercolor as painted from the same field sketch, there are two oils of this subject yet to be found.

In the Peabody Museum there is quite a finished pencil sketch, bearing the legend "Miss. River 700 miles above St. Louis," in which the bluffs on both sides are identical with those of no. 40. In the foreground, instead of two deer, we see a raft being pulled ashore. In the watercolor Mount Trempealeau is the first bluff on the left as we look downstream. The view is a little farther down the river than in no. 39, but not much, for the three bluffs beyond Trempealeau are clearly the same in both pictures. See also nos. 39, 41, 42, and 43.

41. *Indian Deputation on their Way to Washington.* Watercolor, 4⁵/₁₆ x 7. St. Louis Art Museum.

Lewis's plate 3 (*Indian Deputation*), as noted earlier (p. 13 above), is with minor variations a duplicate of this watercolor. In the album Lewis captioned this sketch "A View of the Miss^pi 130 miles above the mouth of the Wisconsin [Prairie du Chien] Indian deputation on their way to Washington." On a pencil study of this same bluff landscape in the Peabody Museum collection Eastman had written: "The mountain that soaks in the water—Miss River. 690 [miles] above St. Louis" (reproduced in McDermott, *Seth Eastman*, plate 58). In *The Valley of the Mississippi Illustrated* (p. 53) Lewis identified "Mount Trompolo [as the bluff] in the distance." The view is upriver.

Eastman's lost oil of this subject, exhibited in St. Louis in Lewis's studio in the spring of 1848 with the title *Deputation of Sioux Indians Near Mount Trempeleau*, pictured "the mountain which 'soaks in the water,' some forty miles below Lake Pepin," according to the *Missouri Republican* of 2 May 1848. The detailed description of the canvas shows the composition to be essentially the same as that of the watercolor (McDermott, *Seth Eastman*, 46).

There are further adventures of Eastman's *Indian Deputation* to be recorded. It has already been noted (p. 8 above) that Lewis as early as 1848 had planned to use this subject as one of the illustrations for his proposed book, but three years after publication of the lithograph (1854) he returned to his model for an oil for the American market. He now painted a 10¼-by-14-inch oil on board, dated on its face 1857, on the back of which many years later he wrote a lengthy title: *On the Upper Mississippi Indian Deputation on their way to Washington Study for a picture painted 1890 by H. Lewis Düsseldorf*. In this version two canoes, each with three Indians, are shown on a sandbar in the foreground; two Indian men with their equipment are about to get into another canoe; a rough, hilly

shore is seen in the background. This picture is now owned by Mr. and Mrs. Eric P. Newman of St. Louis.

The phrase "painted in 1890" seems to imply that in this year he did a larger canvas from the study; if so, the location of it is unknown today. However, in 1857 he sent to New York an oil entitled *On the Upper Mississippi—Indians Embarking*, of which he wrote from Düsseldorf to his brother George in St. Louis: "The picture of the Upper Mississippi I painted from the sketch by Capⁿ Eastman, but I have alter'd it so much that it cannot be call'd a copy. The figures are by [Charles] Wimar." In a later letter (30 June 1863) he gave the title of this still unsold painting as *View on the Upper Miss[iss]ippi. Sunset. Indians Embarking* and the size as 20 by 30 inches (Henry Lewis Papers, Clements Library). The location of this variation of the Eastman subject is unknown.

For other views of Mount Trempealeau see nos. 39, 40, 42, and 43.

42. *Indian Battle Scene   Scalping*. Watercolor, 4⅜ x 7. Duncan Family.

Below this picture in the album Lewis wrote: "Indian Battle Scene"; in the "List": "Scalping—Battle Sious & Chippewas"; on the verso: "Indian

Battle Scene Scalpting by Lt. Col. E. Eastman U.S.A." Plate 29 in his book (an exact copy of the watercolor) is titled *Scalping Scene on the Mississippi*. In *The Valley of the Mississippi Illustrated* (p. 173) he declared that the "Two hills in the background . . . are known as *Cap-à-l'Ail* and *Cap-aux-Puants*." Miss Heilbron objects and I think rightly. Not merely is there no resemblance between the scenery in no. 42 and that in no. 52 (*Mount Cap-à-l'Ail*), but the pages devoted by Lewis to the subject of scalping are included in a chapter on Chippewa customs, and Lewis quoted there from Mrs. Eastman's account of the Sioux (*Dahcotah*, xx). The scene of 42 could not have been as far south as Cape Garlic. The bluff in the center distance of the watercolor is certainly Mount Trempealeau; the view is essentially the same as that in no. 41 but a little farther downstream. See also nos. 39, 40, 41, and 43.

43. *Mount Trempe à l'eau by Moonlight from a point two miles below Looking North*. Watercolor, 4⅜ x 7. St. Louis Art Museum.
      Lewis's caption. The mountain is seen in the right distance. The hills more prominently centered (on the western bank) are presumably Catlin's Rock

(identified in *The Valley of the Mississippi Illustrated*, p. 53, as the site of present-day Richmond, Winona County, Minnesota) and the bluffs Lewis named for himself and his companion John S. Robb of the St. Louis *Reveille*, on the panorama sketching trip in 1848. Dr. Francis Lynch of St. Paul, Minnesota, owns a day-time watercolor of the same view, without the foreground shoreline and encampment.

44. *65 miles above Prairie du Chien on the Miss[issippi] Looking North*. Watercolor, 4⅜ x 7. St. Louis Art Museum.
      Lewis captioned this "Above Prairie du Chien (15 miles)." But in the Minneapolis Public Library sketchbook a watercolor of the same scene (dated 1848) bears the legend I have used.

45. *60 miles above Prairie du Chien looking North*. Watercolor, 4⅜ x 7⅛. St. Louis Art Museum.
      Lewis captioned this "25 Miles above Prairie du Chien." I have taken my title from an 1848 pencil drawing in the Minneapolis Public Library sketchbook.

46. *Sixty Miles above Prarie du Chean*. Watercolor, 4⅜ x

7. *Duncan Family.*
   Lewis's caption in the album.

47. *On the Miss[iss]ippi 40 miles above P[rairie] Du Chien.* Watercolor, 4⅜ x 7. Duncan Family.
    Lewis's caption in the album.

48. *About 25 miles above Prairie du Chien. looking North.* Watercolor, 4⅜ x 7⅛. Duncan Family.
    Lewis located this scene "Ten Miles above Prarie Du Chaen." I take my title from what I think is the original pencil drawing (1848) in the Minneapolis Public Library sketchbook.

49. *About 20 miles above Prairie du Chien Looking North.* Watercolor, 4⅜ x 7. St. Louis Art Museum.
    In the album Lewis captioned this sketch "On the Miss. 30 miles above Prarie Du Chain. Indians moving to new camp." My title is from an 1848 pencil drawing in the Minneapolis Public Library sketchbook. There the bluff view is the same, but the foreground scene of Indian interest is added in the watercolor. It is to be noted that the same figures in the same poses, with very minor differences, have been used before in no. 23 above. Lewis copied no.

58

49 (again with only the slightest alterations) in an oil 19¾ by 27⅞ inches, at present owned by Hirschl & Adler Galleries, New York. In the lower right corner of the canvas Lewis wrote: "Upper Mississippi River 1855."

50. *View 18 miles above Prairie du Chien.* Watercolor, 4⁵⁄₁₆ x 7. Duncan Family.
    In the album Lewis captioned this picture "This View is but two miles below the No. 42 [i.e., 49]." I have adjusted the distance accordingly.

51. *10 Miles above Prairie du Chien looking North.* Watercolor, 4⁵⁄₁₆ x 7. St. Louis Art Museum.
    Lewis's caption was "View 600 miles above St Louis. Indian Hunter." But in the Minneapolis Public Library sketchbook I find a wash drawing (1847) with the same bluff background from which I take my title. The foreground with the Indian shooting has been added in the watercolor.

52. *Mount Cap-à-l'Ail.* Watercolor, 4½ x 7⅛. Duncan Family.
    Lewis wrote on this sketch: "Mount Cap-i-la (Cape Garlic) on the right bank of the Miss." The shape

of the bluff (the pointed one at the river's edge in the center of the view) is known from other pictures of it (e.g., Dana, *The United States Illustrated*, 94). In his *Journal of a Canoe Voyage* (p. 39) Lewis called it "Cap o lange or iron hill"; in *The Valley of the Mississippi Illustrated* (p. 173) he spoke of it as "Cap-a-l'Ail." The latter term has sometimes been explained as "Wing Hill, from the supposed resemblance of its outline to the *wing* of a bird" (Dana, 94). Dana added that it was also known as "*Cap à garlic* [*sic!*], because of the abundance of wild onions found in the valley below." Dana's double confusion arose from the French words *aile* (wing) and *ail* (garlic). Cape Garlic was a few miles above Prairie du Chien, on the east (left) bank of the Mississippi.

53. *Fort Crawford, Prairie du Chien, in 1829*. Watercolor, 4⁷⁄₁₆ x 7¹⁄₁₆. St. Louis Art Museum.

Lewis's plate 30 (*Prairie du Chien, Wisconsin, in 1830*) is an exact copy. Both this date and that he imposed on the watercolor (1847) are wrong, for the finished pencil drawing from which Eastman painted the watercolor is in the Peabody Museum. The inscription on it reads: "Miss. River   Fort Crawford

Prairie du Chien   557 Miles above St. Louis   Oct. 1829" (reproduced in McDermott, *Seth Eastman*, plate 11). The foreground in no. 53 is added. The Peabody also has a rough pencil drawing so dated which is slightly variant in details. Carl S. Dentzell has another finished pencil sketch of the same view. About 1901 Lewis painted from no. 53 an oil with only very slight differences in composition; it is owned by the Minnesota Historical Society (reproduced in Heilbron, *Making a Motion Picture in 1848*, facing p. 39). The fort in this watercolor is the wood structure, 340 feet square with blockhouses at the southeast and northwest corners, built in 1816, which was succeeded by the stone fort begun in the summer of 1829 and completely finished in 1834 (Scanlan, *Prairie du Chien*, 122–154). Faintly seen in the right distance is a large structure, the first portion of the new fort. In 1900 Lewis painted from this sketch an oil now in the Minnesota Historical Society.

54. *View of Prairie du Chien looking North*. Watercolor, 4¼ x 7. Minnesota Historical Society.

Lewis captioned this "View of Prairie Du Chien from the Site of the New Fort looking North."

59

That is, the artist was standing near the new fort looking back upriver, a view almost the reverse of no. 53. The log fort can be seen faintly in the left distance. A slight rough pencil sketch of this scene was in the possession of M. Knoedler & Company about 1960.

55. *On the Miss[issippi] 540 miles above St. Louis 1847.* Watercolor, 4½ x 7⅛. Duncan Family.
My title is from the legend in Eastman's hand in the lower right corner of the watercolor. Lewis cited the same distance. According to Eastman's mileages this scene would be seventeen miles below Prairie du Chien.

56. *Cassville, Wisconsin, in 1829.* Watercolor, 4⅜ x 7⅛. St. Louis Art Museum.
Lewis's plate 32, same title, is an exact copy. Below this sketch in the album Lewis had written: "Cassville in 1848," an obvious error.

57. *Cassville from a Point Two Miles Below.* Watercolor, 4⅜ x 7 1/16. St. Louis Art Museum.
Lewis's album caption.

58. *Near the Mouth of the Fever River.* Watercolor, 4½ x 7. Duncan Family.
Lewis's album caption.

59. *Four Miles below the Mouth of Fever River.* Watercolor, 4⅜ x 7. St. Louis Art Museum.
Lewis's album caption.

60. *Fort Armstrong on the Mississippi—in 1848.* Watercolor, 4½ x 7½. Duncan Family.
Lewis's plate 43 (*Fort Armstrong on Rock Island*) is an exact copy. The Peabody Museum has two rough pencil sketches of the fort made in September 1841, one of which is very like no. 60. The Peabody drawing captioned "Miss. River—Fort Armstrong, Rock Island 357 miles above St. Louis Oct. 1848" (reproduced in McDermott, *Seth Eastman*, plate 60) is a different view taken on the passage to St. Louis. An oil of Fort Armstrong, painted by Lewis about 1900, now in the Minnesota Historical Society, is based at least in part on this Eastman watercolor.

61. *A Prairie on the Miss[issippi] above Montrose.* Watercolor, 4½ x 7⅛. Duncan Family.
Lewis's caption in the album. Montrose is about ten miles above Keokuk on the Iowa side and nearly opposite Nauvoo.

62. *View from Montrose Looking South.* Watercolor, 4½ x 7⅛. Duncan Family.

Lewis's caption in the album. With the single exception of the position of the sawyer (?) bobbing up in the center of the view, this watercolor is exactly like a pencil drawing in the Peabody Museum bearing the legend "View from the Steamboat at Montrose (Iowa) looking down—Sept 2 [21?] 1841 No. 320."

63. *Nauvoo, the Mormon City, in the Distance.* Watercolor, 4½ x 7⅛. Duncan Family.

Lewis's complete caption read: "Nauvoo, the Mormon City in the Distance as It Appeared in 1837." Since the town was not founded until 1839, perhaps he should have written *1847*. The glimpse one gets of Nauvoo is distant and faint.

64. *View of the Prairie at Montrose Looking North near Nauvoo City.* Watercolor, 4¼ x 7. Minnesota Historical Society.

Eastman used this scene for an oil *Landscape with Figure on Horseback—The Prairie Opposite Nauvoo* (reproduced in McDermott, *Seth Eastman*, plate 44), now in the possession of the Minnesota Historical Society. It was painted in 1848 and was declined by the American Art Union in 1849. The trees on the left slope toward the left in the oil; a man on horseback is seen coming up the hill in place of the seated man and the cows in the watercolor. There are some variations in the farms in the distance. But the oil is certainly based on the same study as the watercolor.

65. *From Keokuk at the Foot of [the] Des Moines Rapids.* Watercolor, 4⁷⁄₁₆ x 7¹⁄₁₆. St. Louis Art Museum.

Signed and dated "S. Eastman U S A. 1848." The wood yard is on the Keokuk (east) bank of the Mississippi.

66. *View taken 1 Mile below La Grange.* Watercolor, 4½ x 7½. Duncan Family.

Lewis's caption in the album. The word "Vignette" in his hand in the lower right corner of the picture indicates a possible use for the sketch in his book (which he did not carry out). La Grange is a town in Lewis County, Missouri, about thirty miles below Keokuk.

67. *Eighty Miles above St. Louis.* Watercolor, 4⅜ x 7. St.

Louis Art Museum.
Lewis's caption.

68. *Moonlight View on the Miss[issippi]* *75 Miles above St. Louis.* Watercolor, 4⅜ x 7. St. Louis Art Museum.
Lewis's caption. His plate 28 (*Indians Hunting Deer by Moonlight*) is an exact copy except that the composition is reversed—a mistake by the lithographer. Lewis used this view to illustrate remarks in *The Valley of the Mississippi Illustrated* on Chippewa hunting customs. Possibly the scene is much farther north but for want of evidence I have placed it here in the sequence.

69. *70 Miles above St. Louis—looking North.* Watercolor, 4¼ x 7. Minnesota Historical Society.
The caption is from the Lewis album. The seated figure appears to be the same as the one in an unfinished watercolor or wash drawing in the Minneapolis Public Library sketchbook.

70. *View Sixty Miles above St. Louis.* Watercolor, 4¹¹⁄₁₆ x 7. St. Louis Art Museum.
Caption from the Lewis album.

71. *30 Miles above St. Louis.* Watercolor, 4⁵⁄₁₆ x 7.

Duncan Family.
Signed and dated "S. Eastman U S A 1847."

72. *Shot Towers at Vide-Poche, 6 miles below St. Louis.* Watercolor, 4½ x 7⅛. St. Louis Art Museum.
The same scene as that in Lewis's plate 63 (*Carondelet*), which, however, was clearly after a sketch by Lewis himself (McDermott, *The Lost Panoramas of the Mississippi*, 130). Eastman's angle of view is slightly different and his sketch is more limited in expanse. Today this is an area of bluff in South St. Louis culminating at Bellerive Park, 5800 south.

73. *The Devil's Bake Oven and the Grand Tower.* Watercolor, 4⁷⁄₁₆ x 7¹⁄₁₆. St. Louis Art Museum.
Heading downstream, the nineteenth-century traveler about 120 miles below St. Louis and about 70 miles above the mouth of the Ohio came to two hazards famous in Mississippi River navigation. The Devil's Bake Oven was a bluff on the Illinois shore opposite the mouth of the Obrazo (Brazeau) River. About one-half mile farther down stood the Grand Tower, sometimes called Tower Rock, in the water near the Missouri shore, nearly opposite to the

present-day town of Grand Tower, Illinois. It was obligatory for every passing landscapist to sketch these rocks.

Lewis had two Eastman watercolors that he captioned confusingly "Devil's Bake Oven. 72 miles above the Mouth of the Ohio" and "The Grand Tower 80 miles above the Mouth of the Ohio." I have re-titled one of these as above, for in it we see both of the rocks. The bluff near the center of no. 73 is the Devil's Bake Oven. Beyond it in midstream and obviously farther down the river we see the Grand Tower. Passing these scenes again in October 1848 on his way to Texas, Eastman made two more drawings of Devil's Bake Oven in which we can also see faintly the Grand Tower (Burkhalter, *A Seth Eastman Sketchbook*, 9). See also no. 74.

74. *The Grand Tower*. Watercolor, 4⅜ x 7⅟₁₆. St. Louis Art Museum.

A much closer view of this famous rock (see no. 73). Eastman made three pencil drawings in October 1848: one looking south, one southwest, and one west (Burkhalter, *A Seth Eastman Sketchbook*, 8–9).

75. *View on the Miss[issippi] 20 miles above the Mouth of the Ohio*. Watercolor, 4⅜ x 7. Duncan Family.
Lewis's caption.

76. *16 Miles above the Mouth of the Ohio*. Watercolor, 4½ x 7⅛. St. Louis Art Museum.
Lewis's caption. Dated 1848 in pencil in the lower right corner.

77. *Near the Mouth of the Ohio*. Watercolor, 4⅜ x 7. Duncan Family.
Lewis's caption.

78. *16 Miles below the Mouth of the Ohio*. Watercolor, 4½ x 7¼. Duncan Family.
Lewis's caption.

79. *20 Miles below the Mouth of the Ohio*. Watercolor, 4⅝ x 7⅛. St. Louis Art Museum.
Lewis's caption.

1. The Falls of St. Anthony

2. Indians Killing Fish. View on the Miss[issippi] River 4 miles above Fort Snelling

3. View below the Falls of St. Anthony Looking down the Mississippi

4. Fort Snelling from 1 Mile Above

5. Fort Snelling in 1848

6. View from Tower at Fort Snelling looking North West

7. View from Tower [at] Fort Snelling looking *up* the [Mississippi] River

8. View from Tower at Fort Snelling Looking West

9. Pilot Knob from Fort Snelling

10. The St. Peters River near its Confluence with the Mississippi

11. The Valley of the St. Peters from Fort Snelling

12. Prairie near the Mouth of the St. Peters. Buffalo Hunt.

13. View on the St. Peters 7 Miles from the Mouth

14. Indian Burial Place near Fort Snelling

15. Indian Graves at the Mouth of the St. Peters

16. Indian Burial

17. Dog Dance of the Sioux Indians

18. Travelling Tents of the Sioux Indians Called a Tepe

19. Permanent Residence of the Sioux Indians

20. Fort Snelling from 2 Miles Below

21. St. Paul, Minnesota

22. Little Crow's Village on the Mississippi

23. Red Rock Prairie.   Indians Embarking

24. Medicine Bottle's Village

25. Red Wing's Village

26. Hill near Red Wing's Village on the Miss[issippi]   looking North

27. View of the Lover's Leap

28. Lover's Leap on the Miss[issippi]   looking North

29. Miss[issippi] River   Lake Pepin from the middle of the Lake   looking South

30. View on the Miss[issippi]—160 Miles above Prairie du Chien

31. On the Miss[issippi] 140 miles above Prairie du Chain.   Indians on the Move

32. View 125 miles above Prairie du Chien

33. View 120 miles above Prairie du Chien

34. Six Miles above Wabasha's Prairie.   Looking North

35. Wabasha's Village at Wabasha's Prairie.   140 miles above Prairie du Chien   looking S. W.

36. Bluff at Wabasha's Prairie

37. Beson's Bluff Opposite Wabasha's Prairie

38. Five Miles above Mount Tremble l'eau—looking South   1848.

39. The Mountain that Soaks in the Water on the Miss[issippi] looking South

40. Landscape with Deer in Foreground

41. Indian Deputation on their Way to Washington

42. Indian Battle Scene   Scalping

43. Mount Trempe à l'eau by Moonlight from a point two miles below   Looking North

44. 65 miles above Prairie du Chien on the Miss[issippi]   Looking North

45. 60 miles above Prairie du Chien   looking North

46. Sixty Miles above Prarie du Chean

47. On the Miss[iss]ippi 40 miles above P[rairie] Du Chien

48. About 25 miles above Prairie du Chien. looking North

49. About 20 miles above Prairie du Chien   Looking North

50. View 18 miles above Prairie du Chien

51. 10 Miles above Prairie du Chien   looking North

52. Mount Cap-à-l'Ail

53. Fort Crawford, Prairie du Chien, in 1829

54. View of Prairie du Chien looking North

55. On the Miss[issippi] 540 miles above St. Louis   1847

56. Cassville, Wisconsin, in 1829

57. Cassville from a Point Two Miles Below

58. Near the Mouth of the Fever River

59. Four Miles below the Mouth of Fever River

60. Fort Armstrong on the Mississippi—in 1848

61. A Prairie on the Miss[issippi] above Montrose

62. View from Montrose Looking South

63. Nauvoo, the Mormon City, in the Distance

64. View of the Prairie at Montrose Looking North near Nauvoo City

65. From Keokuk at the Foot of [the] Des Moines Rapids

66. View taken 1 Mile below La Grange

67. Eighty Miles above St. Louis

68. Moonlight View on the Miss[issippi]   75 Miles above St. Louis

69. 70 Miles above St. Louis—looking North

70. View Sixty Miles above St. Louis

71. 30 Miles above St. Louis

72. Shot Towers at Vide-Poche, 6 miles below St. Louis

73. The Devil's Bake Oven and the Grand Tower

74. The Grand Tower

75. View of the Miss[issippi] 20 miles above the Mouth of the Ohio

76. 16 Miles above the Mouth of the Ohio

77. Near the Mouth of the Ohio

78. 16 Miles below the Mouth of the Ohio

79. 20 Miles below the Mouth of the Ohio

Sources Consulted

Manuscripts

Charles Lanman Papers, Library of Congress

Henry Lewis Papers, Clements Library, University of Michigan, Ann Arbor

Henry Lewis Papers, Minnesota Historical Society, St. Paul

Henry Lewis Papers in the collection of the late Mrs. Emilie K. Greenough, privately owned

Unpublished Pictorial Material

Bushnell Collection of Seth Eastman sketches and watercolors in the Peabody Museum, Harvard University

Seth Eastman sketchbook in the Minneapolis Public Library

Published Material

Burkhalter, Lois W. *A Seth Eastman Sketchbook.* San Antonio: Marion Koogler McNay Institute, 1961.

Bushnell, David I., Jr. *Seth Eastman: The Master Painter of the North American Indian.* Smithsonian Institution Miscellaneous Collections, vol. 87, no. 3. Washington, 1932.

————. *Sketches by Paul Kane in the Indian Country, 1845–1848.* Smithsonian Institution Miscellaneous Collections, vol. 99, no. 1. Washington, 1940.

Dana, Charles A., ed. *The United States Illustrated; in Views of City and Country, with Descriptive and Historical Texts.* Vol. I: *The West; or the States of the Mississippi Valley and the Pacific* [engraved half title reads: *The West* and *The Mississippi Valley Illustrated*]. New York: Hermann J. Meyer, [1853–54].

Densmore, Frances. *The Collection of Water-Color Drawings of the North American Indian by Seth Eastman in the James Jerome Hill Reference Library Saint Paul.* St. Paul: John James Hill Reference Library, 1954.

Eastman, Mrs. Mary H. *The American Aboriginal Portfolio. Illustrated by S. Eastman, U.S. Army.* Philadelphia: Lippincott, Grambo and Company, 1853.

———. *Chicora and Other Regions of the Conquerors and the Conquered*. Philadelphia: Lippincott, Grambo and Company, 1854.

———. *Dahcotah; or, Life and Legends of the Sioux around Fort Snelling*. New York: John Wiley, 1849.

Ewers, John C. "George Catlin, Painter of Indians and the West." *Smithsonian Institution Annual Report for 1955*, 483–528. Washington, 1956.

Gayler, Charles. *A Description of Lewis' Mammoth Panorama of the Mississippi River, from the Falls of St. Anthony to the City of St. Louis*. Cincinnati, 1849.

"A Group of Water Colors by Seth Eastman." *City Art Museum of St. Louis Bulletin*, May–June, 1971, pp. 3–7.

Heilbron, Bertha L. *Making a Motion Picture in 1848: Henry Lewis' Journal of a Canoe Voyage from the Falls of St. Anthony to St. Louis*. St. Paul: Minnesota Historical Society, 1936.

———. "Sources of Northwest History: Seth Eastman's Water Colors." *Minnesota History*, XIX, 419–423 (Dec., 1938).

———, ed. *The Valley of the Mississippi Illustrated*. St. Paul: Minnesota Historical Society, 1967.

Johnson, Lila M. "Seth Eastman Water Colors." *Minnesota History*, XLII, 258–267 (Fall, 1971).

Lanman, Charles. *A Summer in the Wilderness*. New York: D. Appleton, 1847.

Lewis, Henry. *Das Illustrirte Mississippithal*. Düsseldorf: Arnz and Company, 1854–57. See also Heilbron, *The Valley of the Mississippi Illustrated*.

McCue, George. "Out of Obscurity." St. Louis *Post-Dispatch*, 13 June 1791, Pictures section, pp. 14–17.

McDermott, John Francis. *The Art of Seth Eastman*. Washington: Smithsonian Institution, 1959.

———. "Charles Deas: Painter of the Frontier." *The Art Quarterly*, XIII, 293–311 (Autumn, 1950).

———. "Henry Lewis and His Views of Western Scenery." *Antiques*, LXI, 332–335 (Apr., 1952).

———. "J. C. Wild: Western Painter and Lithographer." *Ohio State Archaeological and Historical Quarterly*, LX, 111–125 (Apr., 1951).

———. "A Journalist at Old Fort Snelling: Some Letters of 'Solitaire' Robb." *Minnesota History*, XXXI, 209–221 (Dec., 1950).

———. *The Lost Panoramas of the Mississippi*. Chicago: University of Chicago Press, 1958.

———. "Samuel Seymour: Pioneer Artist of the Plains and the Rockies." *Smithsonian Institution Annual Report for 1950*, 497–509. Washington, 1951.

————. *Seth Eastman, Pictorial Historian of the Indian.* Norman: University of Oklahoma Press, 1961.

————. "Some Rare Western Prints by J. C. Wild." *Antiques*, LXXII, 452–453 (Nov., 1957).

Ross, Marvin C. "Footnote to Indian Iconography." *Antiques*, LXXII, 454–455 (Nov., 1957).

St. Louis *Missouri Republican*, 1848.

St. Louis *Weekly Reveille*, 1848.

Scanlan, Peter Lawrence. *Prairie du Chien: French-British-American.* [Menasha, Wis.], 1937.

Schoolcraft, Henry Rowe. *Historical and Statistical Information Respecting the History, Condition and Prospects of the Indian Tribes of the United States.* 6 vols. Philadelphia: Lippincott, Grambo and Company, 1851–57.

[Smith, John Rowson]. *Professor Risley and Mr. J. R. Smith's Original Gigantic Moving Panorama of the Mississippi River.* London, 1849.

Index